Anonymus

Plutarch's Lives: abridged from the original Greek

Anonymus

Plutarch's Lives: abridged from the original Greek

ISBN/EAN: 9783741182136

Manufactured in Europe, USA, Canada, Australia, Japa

Cover: Foto ©Andreas Hilbeck / pixelio.de

Manufactured and distributed by brebook publishing software (www.brebook.com)

Anonymus

Plutarch's Lives: abridged from the original Greek

PLUTARCH's LIVES,

Abridged from the

ORIGINAL GREEK,

Illustrated with

NOTES and REFLECTIONS,

And embellished with

COPPER-PLATE PRINTS.

VOLUME the THIRD.

Containing the LIVES of

PELOPIDAS,	PHILOPOEMEN,
MARCELLUS,	T. Q. FLAMINIUS,
ARISTIDES,	AND
CATO THE CENSOR,	PYRRHUS.

LONDON:
Printed for J. NEWBERY, at the Bible and
Sun, in St. Paul's Church-yard.

MDCCLXII.

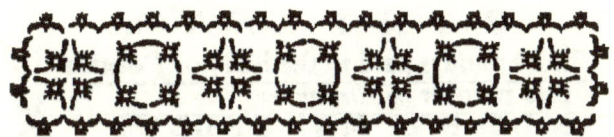

CONTENTS.

THE LIFE of PELOPIDAS Page 1
The characters of *Pelopidas* and *Epaminondas* compared 3
Their behaviour at the battle of *Mantinea* 4
Phœbidas, a *Spartan* commander, seizes *Thebes*, and commits the government into the hands of *Archias* and *Leontidas* 5
Pelopidas and his friends restore the liberty of the *Thebans* 7
The *Athenians* desert the interest of the *Thebans*, but *Pelopidas*, by an artifice, makes them enter into a new alliance 13
Pelopidas and *Epaminondas* obtaining many victories over the *Lacedæmonians*, deprive them of their empire both by sea and land ib.
Pelopidas endeavours to render *Alexander*, the tyrant of *Pheræ*, more just and humane 22
He puts an end to the disputes between *Alexander* king of *Macedon*, and his brother *Ptolomy* ib.
He is taken prisoner by *Alexander* tyrant of *Pheræ*; but *Epaminondas* causes him to be released 24
He is sent ambassador into *Persia* 27
He routs the forces of *Alexander*, tyrant of *Pheræ*, but is slain in the battle 29

CONTENTS.

The honours paid to the body of *Pelopidas* 30
The murder of *Alexander* 33
The LIFE of MARCELLUS 35
A general character of *Marcellus* ib.
The *Romans*, to appease the gods, bury alive two *Greeks*, and two *Gauls* 37
Marcellus kills the king of the *Gauls* with his own hand, dedicates his spoils to *Jupiter Feretrius*, and obtains a complete victory 39
Marcellus is allowed the honour of a triumph 41
His generous behaviour to *Bandius* 43
He puts the *Carthaginians* under *Hannibal* to flight 45
He again defeats *Hannibal* 47
Being desirous of ransoming the *Romans*, who had been made prisoners at the battle of *Cannæ*, he is refused by the senate 48
Marcellus takes *Leontium* in *Sicily* 49
He lays siege to *Syracuse*, but his batteries and his ships are continually destroyed by *Archimedes* ib.
Despairing of success, he leaves *Appius* before that city, ravages *Sicily*, and defeats *Hippocrates* 53
Returning to the siege of *Syracuse*, he takes that city by surprise 54
The unhappy fate of *Archimedes* 55
The extraordinary method taken by *Nicias* to escape from the city of *Enguium* 57
Marcellus taking the finest paintings and statues he found in *Sicily*, to adorn his triumph,

CONTENTS.

triumph, introduces at *Rome* a love of the fine arts 58

Some *Syracusans*, by the persuasion of his enemies, come to *Rome* to lay to his charge several unjust and cruel actions; but this affair ends greatly to his honour 60

He takes the principal cities of the *Samnites*, and opposes *Hannibal* with extraordinary success 62

Marcellus fights *Hannibal* two days successively; and his troops being on the last thrown into disorder, he animates them with fresh courage, and engaging again the next morning, puts the *Carthaginians* to flight 64

Marcellus retiring into *Campania*, to recover and refresh his troops, is accused at *Rome* of leaving the seat of war to go to the baths; however, he is not only acquitted, but a fifth time chosen consul 67

Marcellus and *Crispinus*, the other consul, are both slain 68

Hannibal causing the body of *Marcellus* to be magnificently adorned and burnt, sends his ashes in a silver urn to his son 70

The lives of *Pelopidas* and *Marcellus* compared 71

The LIFE of ARISTIDES 74

The early competition between him and *Themistocles* 75

His moderation, disinterestedness and integrity 76

He resigns the command of the forces to *Miltiades*, and by his bravery contri-

CONTENTS.
butes to their gaining the battle of *Marathon* 78
He is left to guard the prisoners and spoils 79
He obtains the appellation of *The Just* 80
Themistocles causes him to be banished by the ostracism *ib.*
The manner in which the ostracism was conducted 81
Xerxes invading *Greece*, *Aristides* is recalled from banishment, when generously sacrificing his private resentment, he comes to *Themistocles*, and offers him his assistance 82
He contributes to the gaining of the battle of *Salamin* 83
His generous behaviour on the great promises made by the *Persians* to the *Athenians*, to induce them to abandon their allies 84
The *Persians* making a second incursion into *Attica*, *Aristides* is sent ambassador to *Sparta*, to hasten the march of the *Lacedæmonian* troops 85
He is general of the *Athenian* forces at the battle of *Platææ*, and by his wisdom and bravery prevents discord among the allies, and contributes to the obtaining of that victory. 86
Aristides prevents the *Athenians* and *Spartans* having recourse to arms, to decide who should have the honour of erecting a trophy 96
Euchidas, a *Platæan*, in one day fetches

CONTENTS.

Aristides causes several laws to be made for the security of *Greece* in general, and an annual sacrifice to be offered by the *Platæans*, in honour of the *Greeks* slain there . 98

Aristides being joined in commission with *Cimon*, they so endear themselves to the confederates, that the *Lacedæmonians* give up to them the supreme command of the united forces 100

The poverty and death of *Aristides* 102

The LIFE of CATO THE CENSOR 105

His birth, person, and accomplishments *ib.*

The poverty of *Manius Carius*, and the discourses of *Nearchus*, a *Pythagorean* philosopher, strengthen his love of temperance . 107

Valerius Flaccus pleased with his character, invites him to dinner, and persuades him to go to *Rome* . 108

He opposes *Scipio* 109

His eloquence procures him the title of the *Roman Demosthenes* 110

His parsimony 111

His selling his slaves when they grew old 112

His frugal management of the public money 113

His style and manner of speaking 114

The government of *Spain Citerior* falling to his lot, he subdues several nations; but being suddenly encompassed by an army of Barbarians, he promises the *Celtiberians* a sum of money, to induce them to come to his assistance. He serves

CONTENTS.

as a tribune under the consul *Marius Acilius* against *Antiochus* 115

Antiochus having taken possession of the Streights of *Thermopylæ*, *Cato* finds out a narrow path, and with great difficulty attacks him in the rear, and puts his troops to flight 117

Cato's zeal in prosecuting offenders 120

He is created Censor 121

His rigid inflexible behaviour in the discharge of that office 123

The people erect his statue in the temple of health 124

He himself educates his son 125

His behaviour to his slaves 126

The methods by which he acquired wealth 127

His enmity to philosophy, and all foreign erudition *ib.*

In his old age he has an intrigue with a young slave, when, finding that it gave offence to his son, he marries 129

He occasions the destruction of *Carthage* 131

His death 133

Aristides and *Cato* compared *ib.*

The LIFE of PHILOPŒMEN 136

His behaviour in his youth *ib.*

He bravely defends *Megalopolis*, when it is seized by *Cleomenes* king of *Sparta* 137

He distinguishes himself in a battle against *Cleomenes*, in which both his thighs are struck through with a javelin 138.

Being made general of the *Achæan* horse, he trains up the youth to war 140

He

CONTENTS.

He kills *Damophantus*, general of the *Elean* horse — ib.
He defeats the *Lacedæmonians*, and kills *Machanidas* tyrant of *Sparta* — 141
At the *Nemæan* games the people in the theatre clap their hands at seeing him enter — 142
Philip king of *Macedon* sends assassins to murder him — 143
The *Bæotians*, who were storming the city of *Megara*, fly at hearing of his approach — ib.
His success on several occasions against *Nabis* tyrant of *Sparta* — ib.
He renders the city of *Sparta* subject to the *Achæans* — 145
The *Spartans* offer him 120 talents, which he refuses to accept — ib.
His behaviour to the *Spartans* on their twice revolting from the *Achæans* — 147
He endeavours to unite the *Achæans* against the *Romans* — ib.
He is taken prisoner by the *Messinians*, and poisoned — 148
The *Achæans* revenge his death — 150

The LIFE of TITUS QUINTUS FLAMINIUS — 152

His general character — ib.
He is chosen consul before he had discharged the previous offices — 153
The war against *Philip* of *Macedon* falling to his lot, he sails to *Epirus* — ib.
A part of his army being conducted to the top of a mountain, the enemy are attacked

CONTENTS.

attacked on all sides, put to flight, and their camp seized 155

He marches thro' *Thessaly*, without suffering the least injury to be done to the inhabitants 157

He engages all *Greece* to submit to him 158

He enters the city of *Thebes* 159

Both *Philip* and *Titus* send ambassadors to *Rome* ib.

Philip obtaining none of his demands, both armies prepare to engage, but *Philip* is deterred by superstitious fears 160

They engage the next day, and *Titus* obtaining a compleat victory, concludes a peace with *Philip*, whom he obliges to quit *Greece* ib.

Titus appearing at the *Isthmean* games, restores liberty to *Greece* ib.

He every where removes the garrisons, and presses the people to conform to their own laws 165

The *Achæans* make him a present of many *Romans*, who had been taken by *Hannibal*, and sold for slaves 166

Antiochus entering *Greece* with a numerous army, *Atilius* is sent against him, and *Titus* being appointed his lieutenant, is on all occasions the friend of the *Greeks*, 167

The *Chalcidians* dedicate to him the most magnificent of their public structures 169

Titus returning to *Rome*, is created censor. 170

He occasions the death of *Hannibal* ib.

Philopœmen and *Titus* compared 173

The

CONTENTS.

The LIFE of PYRRHUS   176

When an infant, he is saved from assassins, and presented to *Glaucus*, king of *Illyria*, who when he is twelve years old places him on the throne of *Epirus*   *ib.*

Being deprived of his kingdom, he distinguishes himself by his bravery in the great battle of *Ipsus*   179

He is sent as an hostage into *Egypt*, and soon after replaced on the throne of *Epirus*, where he associates *Neoptolemus* with him in the kingdom   180

Neoptolemus contriving to poison him, he causes him to be slain   *ib.*

He restores *Alexander* to the throne of *Macedon*   *ib.*

Demetrius having murder'd *Alexander*, makes war on *Pyrrhus*, but after some losses, concludes a peace with him   182

Demetrius having injured *Pyrrhus*, he invades his kingdom, and is chosen king of *Macedon*   184

Pyrrhus to prevent a war, shares that kingdom with *Lysimachus*; but is soon obliged to resign his part, and return to *Epirus*   187

The *Tarentines* being at war with the *Romans*, invite *Pyrrhus* to be their general   189

A conversation between *Pyrrhus* and *Cineas*   190

Pyrrhus is in great danger at sea from a storm   192

He endeavours in vain to dispute with the *Romans* the passage of the river *Siris* 194

He

CONTENTS.

He defeats the *Romans* in a pitched battle 195

He offers the vanquished *Romans* terms of peace, which are rejected 198

Pyrrhus endeavours to gain the friendship of *Fabricius* 200

Pyrrhus's physician offering to poison his master, *Fabricius* sends the letter to *Pyrrhus* 202

Pyrrhus, unable to procure a peace, comes to an engagement with the *Romans* two days successively, and in the last obtains the victory *ib.*

Ambassadors from *Sicily* desiring him to expel their tyrants, he sails thither, and gains many victories: but his behaviour to the *Sicilians* ruins his affairs 204

He goes to the assistance of the *Samnites* and *Tarentines:* is defeated at sea, but landing in *Italy*, routs a body of the *Mamertines* 207

He is defeated by the *Romans* 208

He returns to *Epirus*; makes war on *Antigonus*, then king of *Macedon*, defeats him, and takes several cities 209

At the desire of *Cleonymus*, he marches to replace him on the throne of *Sparta*, and attacks that city 210

The courageous behaviour of the *Spartan* women 211

Being obliged to retire, he is invited to defend *Argos*. He marches thither, and is slain in that city 213

The behaviour of *Antigonus* on this occasion 216

THE

THE LIFE OF *PELOPIDAS*.

I T is said that in the army of king *Antigonus*, was a soldier, who, tho' he had an unhealthful complexion, distinguished himself by his uncommon bravery, on which the king ordered his physicians to take him under their care, and to spare no pains for his cure. The soldier was soon perfectly recovered from a very painful disease; but with the return of his health, he lost his contempt of danger, when *Antigonus*, to his great surprize, finding him less daring in battle, reproached him

him with the change, on which the soldier replied, "You, Sir, are the cause of my be-
"ing less desperate than before, by deliver-
"ing me from that misery which rendered
"life a burthen." Indeed there is no virtue in behaving with the greatest seeming intrepidity, when that only proceeds from an aversion to life: nor is there any disgrace in endeavouring to avoid death, when it may be done without shame or dishonour. Hence the *Grecian* legislators punished any one who threw away his shield, though they excused the loss of a sword or spear; to intimate that self-preservation, especially in the general of an army, or the governor of a city, is to be preferred to hurting an enemy. For if, like *Iphicrates*, we compare the light-armed troops to the hands, the cavalry to the feet, the main body to the breast, the general to the head, that general who suffers himself to be carried too far by his martial ardour, not only hazards his own person, but the lives of all whose safety depends on his. Indeed where the success can only be expected from the general's exposing himself, he ought not to spare his person; but to exert himself to the utmost, without paying the least regard to the maxims of those who pretend, that a general ought to die of old age. But where a victory would be attended with only an inconsiderable advantage, and a defeat with destructive consequences, none should desire him to perform the part of a common soldier, by hazarding the loss of a general.

. This

PELOPIDAS.

This I thought proper to premise before the lives of *Pelopidas* and *Marcellus*, great men, who perished by their rashness; for each having done honour to his country by his glorious exploits, ventured too far, and threw away their lives when their country most wanted such brave men, and such skilful commanders.

Pelopidas was descended from a noble family in *Thebes* [*], and was brought up in plenty and opulence. To shew that he was not a slave to his riches, he, on his early possessing a large estate, made it his business to relieve the indigent and deserving; but though others thankfully partook of his bounty, *Epaminondas* was the only one among his friends that could not be prevailed on to share his wealth: on which *Pelopidas* condescending to stoop to his poverty, took a pleasure in wearing ordinary apparel, in the frugality of his table, and in his unwearied labour.

Though *Epaminondas* was also of a noble family, yet poverty was familiar and hereditary to him; and he rendered it still more easy, by philosophy and the uniform simplicity of his life. *Pelipidas* married into a good family, and had many children, yet continu-

---

[*] This was a city of *Achaia* in *Greece*, now a province of *Turky* in *Europe*. It was situated near the place where *Thiva* now stands, and ought not to be confounded with *Thebes* in upper *Egypt*, of which a curious description may be seen in The *World Displayed*, Vol XII. pag. 145—165.

ed indifferent with respect to wealth, notwithstanding the encrease of his expences; and by spending his time in the service of the public, impaired his estate. He and *Epaminondas* had naturally the same virtuous dispositions; but *Pelopidas* was fonder of bodily exercises, and *Epaminondas* of the improvements of the mind; so that the one spent all his leisure time in hunting, and wrestling; the other in the study of philosophy and learned conversations: but they were chiefly celebrated for that strict friendship, which they inviolably preserved through the whole course of their lives, without the least spark of that jealousy and envy, which subsisted between *Themistocles* and *Aristides, Cimon* and *Pericles, Nicias* and *Alcibiades*. The virtue of *Pelipodas* and *Epaminondas* preserving them from aiming at wealth and fame, they were equally inflamed with a noble ardour for rendering their country prosperous and happy, and considered each other's success as their own.

According to most authors, this strict friendship did not begin till the battle of *Mantinea*[*], in which the *Thebans* succoured the *Lacedæmonians*, then their friends and allies, against the *Arcadians*. In that battle they fought near each other in one of the wings of the *Lacedæmonian* infantry; and that wing be-

[*] This battle ought not to be confounded with the battle of *Mantinea*, in which *Epaminondas* lost his life, fighting against the *Lacedæmonians*.

ing broken, they joined their shields, and bravely repulsed all that attacked them; till *Pelopidas*, after receiving seven large wounds, fell on a heap of friends and enemies. Tho' *Epaminondas* believed him slain, he stept before him to defend his body and arms, and long maintained his ground against great numbers of *Arcadians*; resolving to die rather than desert his companion, and leave him in the power of the enemy; but being wounded in his breast by a spear, and in his arm by a sword, he was disabled and ready to fall, when *Agesipolis*, king of the *Spartans*, coming unexpectedly to their relief, saved both their lives.

The *Lacedæmonians* after this battle treated the *Thebans* as friends and allies, though they were realy jealous of their encreasing power. In particular they conceived an aversion to the party of *Ismenias* and *Androclides*, in which *Pelopidas* was associated, from their thinking them too zealous for liberty and a popular government. At length *Archias*, *Leontidas* and *Philip*, three rich and ambitious *Thebans*, proposed to *Phœbidas*, a *Spartan* commander, who was marching by *Thebes* with a body of troops, to seize the castle, and put the government into the hands of the nobility. This proposal being approved, *Phœbidas* made himself master of the castle during the feast of *Ceres*, when the *Thebans* little expected any act of hostility. *Ismenias* was taken, and soon after put to death; but *Androclides*, *Pelopidas*, and many others fled, on which they were condemned to perpetual banishment. Mean while *minondas* still remaining at *Thebes*, was disregarded as one who, from his fondness for philosophy and his poverty, had no inclination to attempt, nor the power to execute any great undertaking.

The *Lacedæmonians* hearing what *Phœbidas* had done, not only deprived him of the command, but fined him an hundred thousand drachmas*, and yet continued to keep a garrison in the castle, tho' all *Greece* was surprized at the ridiculous absurdity of punishing the actor, and yet authorizing and confirming the action. The *Thebans* having thus lost their ancient form of government, were enslaved by *Archias* and *Leontidas*, and had no hopes of being freed from a tyranny supported by the *Spartans*; as their yoke could only be broken by a power capable of depriving them of the superiority they enjoyed both by sea and land.

Leontidas hearing that the exiles had retired to *Athens*, where they were kindly received, dispatched after them some assassins, who murdered *Androclides*, but all the rest escaped. The *Athenians* also received letters from *Lacedæmon*, exhorting them to expel the exiles, as the common enemies of *Greece*. But the *Athenians* thought themselves obliged to make a grateful return to the *Thebans*, for the assistance they had given them in restoring their democracy.

* About two thousand and twenty pounds sterling.

But though *Pelopidas* was then very young, he privately spoke to every exile, and often in their public meetings represented the dishonour of neglecting their enslaved and captive country, while they ought to run every hazard in so glorious a cause, taking courage from the example of *Thrasybulus*; for as he marched from *Thebes*, and broke the power of the tyrants in *Athens*, they ought to march from *Athens*, and deliver *Thebes*. Being persuaded by this discourse, they sent secretly to *Thebes* to inform their friends of their designs, which they highly approved. *Charon*, a person of great distinction in the city, offered to receive them in his own house. *Philidas*, another of the party, found the means of being made secretary to *Philip* and *Archias*, who were then Polemarchs, and *Epaminondas* had all along taken pains to inspire the youth with courage and magnanimity.

The day being fixed, the exiles agreed that *Pherenicus* with the rest, should stay at *Thriasium* *, while some of the young men should endeavour to get into the city, and if they were killed, the others should provide for their familes. *Pelopidas* offered to be of the party, and after him *Melon*, *Damoclidas* and *Theopompus*, all persons of the greatest families in *Thebes*, and intimate friends. The whole number amounted to twelve, who taking leave of their companions, set forward meanly dressed, taking with them hounds,

* A little town not far from *Thebes*.

and each carrying a staff in his hand, that they might be taken by those that met them on the road, for hunters straggling about in pursuit of game. Before they came to the city, they separated, and entered at different places. As it was the beginning of winter, the falling snow and a sharp wind, which made most of the citizens stay in their houses, contributed to their passing undiscovered, and being received by those who were in the secret, they immediately went to *Charon*'s house, where being joined by the others, they altogether amounted to forty eight.

Mean while *Philidas*, secretary to the tyrants, who, as hath been already observed, was an accomplice, was giving an entertainment at his own house to *Archias* and his friends, and had promised to provide some women of pleasure to meet them there. But they had not been long at table before a rumour was spread among them, that the exiles were concealed in the city. *Philidas* endeavoured all in his power to divert the discourse: but *Archias* sent an officer to *Charon* to command his immediate attendance.

As it was now growing dark, *Pelopidas* and his friends had put on their armour, and were preparing for action, when they were suddenly alarmed by a loud knocking at the door, and were presently informed, that an officer was come with an order to bring *Charon* to *Archias*. Struck at this news, every one believed that the plot was discovered, and that they should all perish without being able to

perform

perform any exploit worthy of their bravery and resolution. They were however unanimously of opinion that *Charon* should boldly obey the order. On which he brought out his only son who was young, but of remarkable strength and beauty, and delivering him to *Pelopidas,* cried, " If you find me a traitor " use this boy as an enemy, and be cruel in " his execution." This behaviour gave them the greatest concern, and entreating him not to imagine that they had the least suspicion of his fidelity, they earnestly besought him to cause his son to be removed to a place of safety, that if he was so happy as to escape the fury of the tyrants, he might one day revenge his friends and his country. But *Charon* cried, " What life, what safety can " be more honourable than dying bravely " with his father, and so many generous " friends?" Then imploring the protection of the gods, and embracing them all, he departed.

Charon as he went along endeavoured to recollect and compose himself, and being come to the house, *Philip* and *Archias* went to him to the door, and enquired, what persons were lately come to town, and were concealed by the citizens? On which *Charon* asked who they meant? and by whom were they concealed? when perceiving that they had no certain knowledge of the affair, he desired them not to give themselves any disturbance about a vain rumour; adding, that he would make the best enquiry he could, as such things

ought

ought not to be neglected. *Philidas* then appearing, commended his prudence, and returning back with *Archias* to the company, drank him up to a high pitch; prolonging the entertainment, by telling them the women were coming.

Scarce was this storm blown over, when an express arrived from *Archias*, high priest of *Athens*, to *Archias* of *Thebes*, his particular friend; and the courier delivering him letters that contained a full and exact account of the whole conspiracy, told him, that the person who wrote them entreated him to read them immediately, as they contained business of the utmost consequence. But *Archias* having drank himself mellow, took the letters, and saying with a smile, *Business to-morrow*, put them under the boulster of the couch, and resumed his conversation with *Philidas*.

Every thing being at length ripe for action, the conspirators issued out, and dividing into two bodies; one under the command of *Pelopidas* and *Damcclidas*, went to the houses of *Leontidas* and *Hypates*, while the others, under the conduct of *Charon* and *Melon*, hasted to attac *Archias* and *Philip*; these wore womens cloaths over their armour, and branches of pine and poplar about their heads to shade their faces. On their entering the room, the whole company shouted for joy, thinking them the women they had so long expected. But the conspirators looking around them to observe who were present, suddenly drew their swords, and attacked *Archias* and *Philip* across the table. By the persuasions of *Philidas*, a few of
the

the guests were induced to sit still; while the rest, who rose up to defend themselves, and assist their chiefs, being intoxicated, were easily dispatched.

Mean while *Pelopidas* and his party going to the house of *Leontidas*, found the doors shut; for he was already gone to bed. They knocked a long time before any body answered: at last, being heard by a servant, he came to the door, but scarce had he unbolted, and half opened it, than rushing in all together, they threw him down, and ran up stairs to *Leontidas*'s chamber. *Leontidas* hearing the noise, leaped out of bed and seized his sword; but forgot to put out the lights, which had he done, they might have fallen foul on each other in the dark, and given him an opportunity of escaping. He received them at the door, and stabbed the first man who attempted to enter. He was then attacked by *Pelopidas*; but the passage being narrow, and the dead body lying between them, they fought a considerable time, till at last *Pelopidas* killed him. They then went in search of *Hypates*, and entered his house in the same manner; but he being alarmed at the noise, escaped to a neighbour's house, when being closely followed, he was overtaken and slain.

This party having thus performed their task, went to join *Melon*; and sending to hasten the exiles they had left in *Attica*, proclaimed liberty to all the *Thebans*. Then taking down the spoils that hung over the porticos, and breaking open the shops of the armourers and
sword-

sword-cutlers, they armed all that came to their assistance. In the mean time *Epaminondas* and *Gorgidas* having assembled and armed a great body of young men, and some of the strongest of the old, came in and joined them.

By this time the whole city was filled with terror and confusion; the houses were full of lights, and the streets of people running backwards and forwards: all were filled with amazement, and knowing nothing with certainty of what had happened, waited impatiently for the day. The *Spartan* garrison, which then consisted of fifteen hundred men, and were besides joined by many of the citizens, were in such consternation at the outcries, numerous lights, and confused hurry of the people, that they did not attempt to move, but were contented with preserving the castle.

Day no sooner appeared than the exiles from *Attica* entered the city in arms, and there was held a general assembly of the people; to which *Epaminondas* and *Gorgidas* brought *Pelopidas* and his party, encompassed by the priests carrying garlands in their hands, and exhorting the people to fight for their gods and their country. At this sight the whole assembly rose up, and with the loudest acclamations received them as the deliverers of their country. *Pelopidas* was appointed governor of *Bœotia*, and he, with *Melon* and *Charon*, immediately blocked up the castle, in order to get possession of it before any succours could arrive from *Sparta:* Indeed he was but
a little

a little before hand with them; for the *Lacedæmonians* had scarce surrendered the place, and according to the capitulation were returning home, when they met *Cleombrotus* marching towards *Thebes* with a powerful army. The three chief commanders were called to an account for signing the capitulation, and for this two of them were executed, and the third so severely fined, that, being unable to pay the sum, he was forced to fly his country.

This action nearly resembles that by which *Thrasybulus* restored the liberty of *Athens*; but it would be difficult to find another instance, in which so inconsiderable a number of men, by their conduct and bravery, overcame such a powerful opposition, and procured such signal advantages to their country: for *Pelopidas*, with his eleven brave companions, without taking a castle, a fortification, or a town, in one night, by entering two or three private houses, freed his country, and broke in pieces the chains of the *Spartan* government, which till then had been thought indissoluble, and gave rise to a war that humbled the pride of the *Spartans*, and deprived them of their empire both by sea and land.

Soon after the *Thebans* had thus recovered their liberty, the *Lacedæmonians* entering *Bæotia* with a powerful army, the *Athenians* were so terrified, that they not only deserted the interest of the *Thebans*, but prosecuted all who continued to favour them; putting some to death, banishing others, and laying a heavy fine on the rest. The affairs of the *Thebans*, who had no friend or ally, now seemed in a desperate situation; but *Pelopidas* and *Gorgidas*, then governors of *Bœotia*, consulting how to produce a fresh quarrel between the *Athenians* and *Spartans*, agreed on the following expedient. *Sphodrius* a *Spartan* of great courage, but always full of vain and ambitious projects, had been left at *Thespæ* with a body of troops to receive and protect such *Bœotians*, as deserting the interest of their country, should join the *Spartans*. To him *Pelopidas* privately sent money, and at the same time such advice as was most proper to flatter his vanity; particularly, that he ought to undertake some noble enterprize, and that as nothing could be so agreeable to the *Spartans* as the conquest of *Athens*, he might make a sudden incursion on the unprovided *Athenians* and surprize the *Piræus*: for the *Thebans*, now hating the *Athenians*, would lend them no manner of assistance. *Sphodrias* persuaded by these reasons, marched by night, and entering *Attica* in an hostile manner, advanced as far as *Eleusis*, but finding his design discovered, returned to *Thespæ*. Immediately upon this the *Athenians* entered into a new alliance with the *Thebans*, and assisted them to the utmost of their power.

Mean while the *Lacedæmonians* were several times defeated by the *Thebans*, not only in several slight skirmishes; but at *Platæa* and *Thespia*, where *Phœbidas*, who had surprized the *Cadmea*, was slain; and at *Tanagra*, where *Pelopidas* slew with his own hand *Panthoides*

their

their commander in chief. In particular the battle of *Tegyræ* raised *Pelopidas*'s reputation very high; for no other commander shared with him in the honour of the day.

Pelopidas keeping a strict eye on the city of *Orchomenus*, which had received a *Spartan* garrison, at length imagined that he had found an opportunity of retaking it. For receiving intelligence that the garrison was marched out to make an incursion into *Locris*, he hasted thither with the sacred battalion and some horse, hoping to find the place defenceless; but when he came near the city, hearing that a body of troops was marching from *Sparta* to reinforce the garrison, he retreated with his little army by *Tegyræ* along the sides of the mountains, the only way he was capable of passing; for all the flat country was overflowed by the river *Melas*, which when it rises, spreads into marshes and navigable pools, rendering all the lower roads impassable. As the *Spartans* were marching at the same time from *Locris*, they had no sooner passed the streights than they appeared in view: on which one running in haste to *Pelopidas*, cried, *We are fallen into the enemy's hands.* To which he calmly answered, *And why not they into ours.* He then ordered the horse, which were in the rear, to advance and begin the attack; and drew up his foot, who amounted to three hundred men, into a close body, having no doubt of their forcing a passage through the enemy, though they were superior in number. The *Spartans* had divided their infantry into two battalions, each consisting, according

cording to *Ephorus* of five hundred, *Callisthenes* says seven hundred, but *Polybius* and others, nine hundred. *Theopompus* and *Gorgoleon* the *Spartan* generals led them to the charge with great bravery. The shock began where the commanders on both sides fought in person, and was very violent: the *Lacedæmonian* generals, who pressed hard on *Pelopidas*, fell first, and all who were near them were either killed or put to flight. The whole army were now so terrified, that they opened to let the *Thebans* pass; but *Pelopidas* disdaining to accept this opportunity of making his escape, turned on those who still kept their ground, and made such a terrible slaughter, that they were soon routed and put to flight. The *Thebans* however did not pursue them very far; but were satisfied with the advantage they had already gained, and with making an honourable retreat, through the remains of a dispersed and defeated army. Having therefore gathered the spoils of the slain, and erected a trophy, they returned home elated with their success: for the *Spartans* in all their former wars were never before beaten by a smaller or even an equal number. Thus this battle first taught the *Greeks*, that neither the *Eurotas**, nor the country situated between *Babyce* and *Cnacion* †, breeds martial spirits and brave warriors; but that wherever the youth are ashamed of what is base, are reso-

---

* A river of *Sparta*.

† Between those towns was situated the territory of *Sparta*.

lutely

lutely virtuous, and fear dishonour more than death, there will be found the men most terrible in arms.

Gorgidas, who first raised the sacred band, in all engagements dispersed the men of which it was composed, in the first ranks of his infantry, which rendered their courage less conspicuous. But *Pelopidas* having thus experienced their astonishing bravery at the battle of *Tegyræ*, where they fought together, ever after kept them entire in one body, and constantly charged at their head in the most difficult attacks. Thus as horses, when harnessed together in a chariot*, proceed with greater spirit and alacrity, so *Pelopidas* thought, that men of bravery striving to excel each other in the pursuit of glory, would fight with redoubled resolution.

The *Lacedæmonians* having at length concluded a peace with all the other *Greeks*, *Cleombrotus* their king entered the country of the *Thebans* with an army of ten thousand foot, and a thousand horse; on which the *Thebans* found themselves in danger not only of again losing their liberty, but of being intirely extirpated. When *Pelopidas* was setting out to join the army, his wife followed him to the door, and earnestly besought him, with many tears, to take

* This doubtless alludes to the chariot races in the public games of *Greece*, in which the horses were all harnessed in a row, and placed a-breast: it was also in the *Roman* triumphs, the four horses that drew the conqueror's chariot were all placed a-breast.

care of himself: but he replied, "Private men are to be advised to take care of themselves, and the commanders to take care of others." On his coming up with the army, he found the general officers divided in opinion, and was the first that joined with *Epaminondas*, who advised giving the enemy battle. He was then captain of the sacred band, and the *Thebans* placed great confidence in him, on account of the signal proofs he had given of his zeal for the liberty of his country.

When the above resolution was taken, both armies lay before *Leuctra* *, and at that time *Pelopidas* had a dream which gave him much uneasiness. Long before the daughters of a person named *Scedasus* had been basely ravished by some *Spartans* whom they had entertained, and being unable to survive the disgrace, had killed themselves, and were interred in the plain of *Leuctra*, whence they were called *Leuctrides*.

Their father, justly enraged, went to *Sparta* to demand satisfaction, for so vile and detestable an action; but being unable to obtain it, he uttered the most dreadful imprecations against the *Spartans*, and then slew himself at his daughters tomb. *Pelopidas* being asleep in his tent, fancied he saw those women weeping at their tomb, and loading the *Spartans* with imprecations; while *Scedasus*, their father, ordered him, if he desired to gain the victory, to sacrifice a young red-

* A small town of *Bœotia* between *Platææ* and *Thispiæ*.

haired

haired virgin to his daughters. *Pelopidas* considering this as a cruel and impious injunction, arose, and told it to the soothsayers and commanders of the army; some of whom thought that the order should not be disobeyed, and alledged many examples in ancient history of such sacrifices being justified by the event. Others, on the contrary, urged that so barbarous an oblation could not be acceptable to any superior being: that the world was not governed by *Typhon* and the giants, but by the Father of gods and men: that it was the greatest absurdity to suppose that the deities delighted in human sacrifices; and even if any of them did, they ought to be neglected as vicious and impotent beings; since such corrupt desires could only subsist in weak and depraved minds. But while the generals were thus differing in opinion, a wild she-colt, that had broke out from the stud, ran through the camp, and stopped near the place where they were. While some were admiring the bright red of her mane, the fineness of her shape, and her spirit and vigour, *Theocritus* the diviner cried to *Pelopidas*, " Behold there the victim that comes to offer herself, wait for no other virgin, but sacrifice that the gods have sent thee." Upon this they seized the colt, and sacrificed her with the usual ceremonies on the tomb of the *Leuctrides*; expressing their joy, and publishing throughout the army *Pelopidas*'s vision, and the sacrifice required.

Epaminondas formed his left wing into an oblique battalion, that by dividing the right wing of the *Spartans* from their allies, he might

might the more easily break them. But the enemy perceiving his design, changed the disposition of their army, and began to extend their right wing, in order to encompass *Epaminondas*: but *Pelopidas* coming briskly up at the head of the sacred band before *Cleombrotus* could close his division, fell on the disordered *Lacedæmonians*. The *Spartans* were indeed the most expert warriers of all the *Grecians*, and were particularly accustomed to preserve their ranks, and unite their efforts in whatever part the danger was most pressing. But now *Epaminondas* falling upon the right wing, while they were in confusion, without offering to attack the other troops, and at the same time *Pelopidas* advancing with incredible speed and bravery at the head of his three hundred men, baffled all their art, and made such slaughter of the *Spartans*, as had never before been known. Thus *Pelopidas*, though he only commanded the sacred band, obtained as much honour by the victory as *Epaminondas* himself, who was commander in chief*.

Pelopidas and *Epaminondas* being joint governors of *Bœotia*, soon after marched into *Peloponnesus*, where they recovered from the *Lacedæmonians Elis, Argos*, all *Arcadia*, and the greatest part of *Laconia*. But it being now the depth of winter the time of their office was near expiring; and as those who refused to deliver up their office were liable to be punished with

* The victory of *Leuctra* was gained in the three hundred and seventieth year before the birth of Christ.

death,

death, the rest of their colleagues, from fear of the law, and to avoid the inclemency of the season, were for speedily marching back to *Thebes*; but *Pelopidas* and *Epaminondas* encouraging their fellow-citizens, marched against *Sparta*, and passing the *Eurotas*, took several towns, ravaging the whole country quite to the sea coast, at the head of an army of about seventy-thousand men, of whom the *Thebans* did not compose a twelfth part. But the distinguished reputation of these two great commanders made all the allies follow and obey them, even without any decree or agreement. For the first and supreme law of nature seems to direct, that when men stand in need of protection, they should chuse such chiefs as are best able to defend them. In their expedition they united all *Arcadia* into one body, and driving out the *Spartans* who inhabited *Messenia*, recalled its ancient inhabitants, and repeopled *Ithome*. Then returning home through *Cenchrea*, defeated the *Athenians*, who had attacked them in the narrow ways in order to prevent their passage.

But while all *Greece* applauded the valour, and admired the success of these great commanders, the envy of their fellow-citizens prepared such a reception for them at their return, as the signal services they had performed for their country very ill deserved; they both being capitally tried for not resigning their command at the appointed time, and holding it four months longer, during which they performed those great actions in *Laconia*, *Arcadia*,

Arcadia, and *Messenia*. *Epaminondas* bore this ill treatment with the greatest patience, for he imagined, that a principal part of true fortitude and magnanimity consisted in his not resenting the injuries done him by his fellow-citizens: but *Pelopidas*, being of a warmer temper, excited his friends to revenge the affront, which they at length did, by causing a heavy fine to be laid on *Meneclides* the principal accuser of these brave commanders.

In the mean time *Alexander*, the tyrant of *Pheræ*, invaded *Thessaly*, upon which the *Thessalians* sending ambassadors to *Thebes*, to desire the assistance of some troops and a general, *Pelopidas* marched thither with an army, and soon reduced the city of *Larissa*. *Alexander* then coming to him in a submissive manner, he endeavoured, by the force of persuasion, to render him more just and merciful; but finding him incorrigible, and receiving daily complaints of his inhumanity, lewdness and avarice, he began to treat him with some severity, on which the tyrant privately escaped with his guards.

Pelopidas, after having thus succoured the *Thessalians*, marched for *Macedonia*, where *Ptolemy* was making war against *Alexander* * king of *Macedon*; he having been invited thither by those two brothers, in order to decide their disputes, and assist the prince who should

---

* *Alexander* with *Perdiccas* and *Philip* were all the legitimate sons of *Amyntas* II. and *Ptolemy* was his natural son.

appear to be injured. *Pelopidas* immediately put an end to all their differences; recalled those who had been banished, and taking *Philip* *, *Alexander*'s brother, with thirty youths of the chief families in *Macedonia* for hostages, carried them to *Thebes*. Thus shewing the *Grecians* the authority the *Thebans* had gained by the reputation of their arms, and the high opinion conceived of their justice and integrity.

The next year the *Thessalians* again complained of *Alexander* the *Pherean*, for disturbing their peace, and forming designs against their cities; upon which *Pelopidas* and *Ismenias* were sent as ambassadors. At the same time fresh commotions happened in *Macedonia*; *Ptolemy* having murdered his brother *Alexander*, and seized his kingdom; the friends of the deceased king sent for *Pelopidas*, who being willing to espouse their interest, immediately raised a body of mercenaries, and marched with them against *Ptolemy*. On their advancing near each other *Ptolemy* found means to corrupt the mercenaries, and prevail on them to go over to him; but fearing *Pelopidas*, came submissively to him; endeavoured to pacify him, and solemnly promised not only to keep the kingdom for the brothers of the deceased king, but to esteem the friends and enemies of *Thebes* as his own; and then gave *Philoxenus*, his son, with fifty of his

* This *Philip* was the father of *Alexander* the Great.

companions

companions as hostages. These *Pelopidas* sent to *Thebes*; but, resenting the treachery of the mercenaries, and hearing that they had left the best part of their effects, together with their wives and children at *Pharsalus*, he resolved to revenge the injury he had received by seizing on them, and assembling some *Thessalian* troops, marched thither. But, he had no sooner reached that city, than *Alexander* the tyrant, appearing before it with a considerable army, *Pelopidas*, thinking he came thither to justify himself, by answering the complaints that had been made against him, went with *Ismenias* to him, without taking any precautions for the security of their persons; upon which the tyrant, seeing them alone and unarmed, took them prisoners, and made himself master of *Pharsalus*.

The *Thebans* were highly incensed at hearing of this outrage, and immediately sent an army into *Thessaly*; and, *Epaminondas* happening to be under their displeasure, they made choice of other generals.

Mean while the tyrant brought *Pelopidas* to *Pheræ*, and thinking that his disaster would humble his spirit, and abate his courage, permitted all that would to see him. But *Pelopidas* advising the complaining *Phereans* to be comforted, assured them, that the tyrant would soon meet with the reward of his crimes, and even sent to let *Alexander* know, that he was guilty of an absurdity, in daily tormenting and putting to death so many innocent and worthy citizens, and yet sparing him,

him, who, he knew, if ever he escaped, would make him suffer the punishment he deserved. Surprized at his boldness, the tyrant asked, *Why is* Pelopidas *in such haste to die?* Which being repeated to *Pelopidas,* the illustrious prisoner replied, *It is because thou may'st the sooner perish, by becoming still more hateful to the gods.*

Though the tyrant forbad any one, from that time, to see or discourse with him, *Thebe* his wife, being informed by his keepers of his great firmness and intrepidity, visited him in his prison, and guessing by the meanness of his dress and provisions, that he was treated very unworthily, burst into tears. As *Pelopidas* did not at first know who she was, he stood amazed; but, on his being told her name, he addressed her by the name of *Jason* her father, who had been one of his intimate friends; and she saying she pitied his wife, he returned, *And I you, who being at liberty, can endure* Alexander. This touched *Thebe* to the quick; for, from the many outrages she had received, she was exasperated against her inhuman husband *.

The

---

* It is said that the tyrant loved her tenderly; but, notwithstanding that tenderness, treated her very cruelly, and was in such perpetual distrust, even of her, that he never went to her apartment without a slave carrying a naked sword before him, and sending a guard to search every coffer for concealed poniards. Wretched prince,

The *Theban* generals, who entered *Theſſaly*, were obliged, either through ill fortune, or bad conduct, to make a diſhonourable retreat; on which the *Thebans* fined each of them ten thouſand drachmas †, and diſpatched *Epaminondas* at the head of an army to repair the diſhonour. The fame and reputation of that wiſe commander, gave freſh life and courage to the *Theſſalians*, and the tyrant's ſubjects being ready to revolt, his affairs ſeemed in a very deſperate ſituation: but *Epaminondas*, preferring the ſafety of *Pelopidas* to his own reputation; and fearing, that if he at firſt puſhed matters to an extremity, the tyrant might grow deſperate, and turn all his fury againſt his priſoners, managed him in ſuch a manner, by hovering about with his army, as not to encreaſe his fierceneſs and cruelty. He knew the little regard he paid to reaſon and juſtice, and was not ignorant that he had cauſed ſome men to be buried alive, and others to be dreſſed in the ſkins of boars and bears, and then baited them with dogs, or ſhot at them for his diverſion. He had ſummoned the inhabitants of *Scotuſa* and *Melibœa*, two cities in friendſhip and alliance with him, to an aſſembly; and, having ſurrounded them with his guards, and them all, both young and old, to the

---

prince, cries *Cicero*, who could confide more in a ſlave and a Barbarian, than in his own wife! *Cic. de Offic.* l. 2.

† About 225 l. ſterling.

sword. He consecrated the spear with which he slew his uncle *Polyphron*, and crowning it with garlands, offer'd sacrifice to it as to a god. But this monster of cruelty, being terrified at the very name and character of *Epaminondas*, hastily dispatched an embassy to offer satisfaction; but that great man refusing to admit him as an ally of the *Thebans*, allowed him only a truce of thirty days; and having recovered *Pelopidas* and *Ismenias*, returned with his army to *Thebes*.

The *Thebans* now discovering, that the *Spartans* and *Athenians* had sent ambassadors to conclude a league with *Artaxerxes* king of *Persia*, sent *Pelopidas* on their part; who no sooner entered the *Persian* dominions, than he was universally honoured, the fame of his victories being every where spread abroad. On his arrival at the *Persian* court, he became the object of the admiration of the nobles and great officers: " This is the man,
" said they, who deprived the *Lacedæmonians*
" of their empire by sea and land, and con-
" fined within the bounds of the *Taygetus* and
" *Eurotas*, that *Sparta*, which a little before,
" under the conduct of *Agesilaus*, made war
" on our great monarch, and threatened the
" kingdoms of *Susa* and *Ecbatana*." Even *Artaxerxes*, being desirous of shewing that persons of the most illustrious characters made their court to him, studied to heighten his reputation by doing him all imaginable honours. But, on his seeing him, and hearing his discourse, which was stronger than that

of the *Athenians*, and plainer than that of the *Spartan* ambassadors, his esteem for him encreased, and he made no secret of the great regard he had entertained for him: the customary presents he sent him were as rich and magnificent as possible, and he granted all his demands, which were, that the *Greeks* should be free and independent, that *Messene* should be repeopled, and the *Thebans* be always esteemed the king's hereditary friends. On his having received so favourable an answer, he returned home, without accepting any other of the presents, than such as served as a pledge of the king's favour.

The esteem and affection of the *Thebans* for *Pelopidas* were greatly encreased by this embassy, in which he procured the re-establishment of *Messene*, and the freedom of *Greece*. At this time *Alexander*, the *Pherean* tyrant, had destroyed several cities of *Thessaly*, and put garrisons into those of the *Pthiotæ*; the *Magnesians* and *Achæans*, who no sooner heard that *Pelopidas* was returned, than they sent deputies to *Thebes*, to desire the assistance of some forces, and him for their general. Their request was instantly granted: but, when *Pelopidas* was just ready to march, the sun was suddenly eclipsed, and the city of *Thebes* was at noon covered with darkness. When seeing his fellow-citizens filled with great consternation at this phænomenon, he was unwilling to hazard the lives of seven thousand of his fellow-citizens, by compelling them to march, while their minds were filled with terror,

terror, but committing himself wholly to the *Theſſalians*, he took only three hundred horſe, compoſed of *Theban* and foreign voluntiers, and, contrary to the opinion of the ſoothſayers, and the reſt of the people, departed. For *Pelopidas* was reſolved to let all the *Grecians* ſee, that, while the *Spartans* endeavoured to ſupport *Dionyſius* the *Sicilian* tyrant, and the *Athenians* were kept in pay by *Alexander*, and had erected a brazen ſtatue to his honour, the *Thebans* alone waged war to ſuccour the diſtreſſed, and to exterminate out of *Greece* all arbitrary power.

Pelopidas having aſſembled his forces at *Pharſalus*, marched againſt the tyrant, who, finding that he had but few *Thebans*, and that his own infantry were above double the number of that of the *Theſſalians*, marched to meet him; when *Pelopidas* being told, that the tyrant was advancing with a prodigious army, "So much the better, ſaid he, we "ſhall beat the greater number." Near *Cynoſcephalæ* are two ſteep hills oppoſite to each other, in the middle of a plain. Both ſides ſtrove to get poſſeſſion of them with their foot; at the ſame time *Pelopidas* ordered his horſe, which were very numerous, to charge the enemy's cavalry, and ſoon routing them, they purſued them over the plain. *Alexander* had, however, gained the hills before the *Theſſalian* foot could reach them, and falling fiercely on thoſe *Theſſalians* who attempted to gain the aſcents, killed the foremoſt of them, and wounded

wounded so many of those that followed, that they were obliged to give way. *Pelopidas*, on seeing this, called back his horse, and taking his shield, made all possible haste to join those that fought about the hills, and advancing to the front, his men seemed inspired with fresh courage. The enemy stood two or three charges; but finding the *Thessalian* foot still press forward, and seeing the horse returning from the pursuit, they began to give ground. *Pelopidas* then mounting an ascent, where he had a view of the enemy's army, cast his eyes around in search of *Alexander*, when perceiving him in the right wing, rallying and encouraging his mercenaries, he became no longer master of himself; but, sacrificing both his safety and his duty as a general, to his passion, advanced far before the soldiers, loudly challenging the tyrant, who, struck with fear, retreated, and hid himself among his guards. The foremost of the mercenaries, that dared to oppose him, were cut down by *Pelopidas*; but others, who fought at a distance, pierced him with their javelins, and mortally wounded him. The *Thessalians*, on seeing his danger, hastened to his assistance; but, on their coming to the place where he was, found him lying dead on the ground. But, at the same time, both the horse and foot pressing hard on the enemy, intirely defeated them, and pursued them far over the plain. The *Thebans* in the army, now expressed the deepest concern at the death of *Pelopidas*, calling him their *father, their saviour, their instructer in every*

every thing great and honourable. This indeed was no wonder; for the *Thessalians* and their allies, by their grief, gave still more evident proofs of their love to him; for the whole army, on hearing that he was dead, neither put off their armour, nor dressed their wounds; but, notwithstanding the heat of the weather, and their fatigue, ran immediately to him, and heaped up the spoils of the enemy around his dead body; then cut off their own hair and their horses manes; and many, on their retiring to their tents, neither kindled a fire, nor took any refreshment. In short, a silent consternation reigned thro' the whole army, as if, instead of having obtained a great and glorious victory, they had been defeated and enslaved.

At every city through which his body was carried, the magistrates, priests, young men, and children, came to meet it with crowns, trophies, and golden armour. The oldest men among the *Thessalians* begged the *Thebans* to allow them to inter it; on which occasion one of them made the following speech:
" Suffer us to ask a favour, that will be a sin-
" gular honour and consolation to us in this
" great misfortune. It is not *Pelopidas* alive
" whom the *Thessalians* desire to attend. It
" is not to *Pelopidas*, sensible of what is done
" to him, that they would pay the honours
" due to his merit. No, all we ask is the
" permission to wash, adorn, and inter his
" dead body; which, if we obtain, we shall
" then be persuaded, that you do us the jus-
" tice

"tice to believe, that our share in this com-
"mon calamity is greater than yours. You,
"'tis true, have lost an excellent general;
"but we, with the loss of a general, have
"lost all hopes of liberty; for how shall we
"presume to desire another of you, when
"we cannot restore *Pelopidas*?" The *Thebans*
granted their request; and never was there
seen a funeral that did such honour to the deceased: for nothing could be more astonishing, than to see a man die in a strange country, where, neither his wife, children, or kinsmen were present, and yet attended, crowned and interred by so many cities striving to exceed each other in the demonstrations of their esteem. *Æsop*'s observation is certainly not true, that " death is most unfortunate in the time of prosperity and success:" for it is then most happy, as it secures to good men the glory of their virtuous actions, and raises them above the power of fortune. Thus *Pelopidas*, after having spent the greatest part of his life in performing the noblest exploits; and, after he had been thirteen times governor of *Bœotia*, died at last in a brave attempt to extirpate tyranny, and restore the liberties of *Thessaly*.

Great as the grief was, which the death of *Pelopidas* occasioned, yet still greater was the advantage the allies received from it; for, it was no sooner known to the *Thebans*, than prompted by a desire of revenge, they sent to their assistance an army of seven thousand foot and seven hundred horse, under the command

of

of *Malcitus*, and *Diogeton*, who, falling upon *Alexander*, who was already much weakened, compelled him to restore the cities he had again taken from the *Thessalians*, to withdraw his garrisons from the *Phthiotæ*, the *Magnesians*, and the *Achæans*, and to take an oath, to afford the *Thebans* at all times whatever assistance they should demand.

The tyrant was however soon punished for his wickedness. *Thebe*, who had been taught by *Pelopidas*, to disregard the exterior shew and pomp of tyranny, fearing the treachery, and hating the cruelty of her husband, conspired with her three brothers, *Tisiphonus*, *Pytholaus*, and *Lycophron*, to murder him. At night the palace was full of guards, except the tyrant's bed-chamber, which was guarded by a dog chained at the door, that would fly at all but the tyrant and his wife, and one slave, who always fed him. The time appointed being come, *Thebe* concealed her brothers all day in an adjacent room; and at night, going alone, as usual, into *Alexander*'s chamber, where she found him asleep, she soon returned, and ordered the slave to lead away the dog, pretending the king had a mind to sleep without being disturbed; and that the stairs might make no noise when her brothers came up, she covered them with wool. She then softly conducted her brothers to the door, where leaving them with poinards in their hands, she went again into the chamber, but soon returned with the tyrant's sword that hung at his bed's head, and shew-

ed

ed it them as a proof of his being fast asleep. The young men however, now appeared struck with terror, and did not dare to proceed; at which *Thebe* was so enraged, that, reproaching them for their cowardice, she swore she would awake her husband, and discover the whole plot. This making them resume their former resolution, she conducted them into the chamber, and, with a light in her hand, led them to the bed; when one of them catching him by the hair of the head, another seized him by the feet, while the other stabbed him with the poinard. His death may perhaps be thought too quick and easy for so cruel a monster; but, if it be considered, that his dead body was exposed to all kinds of indignities, and spurned and trampled under foot by his own subjects, his punishment may appear to bear some proportion to his crimes.

THE LIFE OF MARCELLUS.

ARCUS *Claudius*, the son of *Marcus*, was the first of his family who obtained the name of *Marcellus*. This great man was naturally hardy, active and intrepid; but his impetuosity and fierceness only appeared in battle; for, on all other occasions, he was remarkably modest, humane, and courteous. Fond of the *Grecian* learning and eloquence, he honoured all that excelled in them. He had an extraordinary skill in all kinds of fighting, especially in single combat,

bat, and never refused a challenge*, or failed of killing those that challenged him. In *Sicily*, once seeing his brother *Otacilius* in danger, he defended him with his shield; slew those by whom he was attacked, and saved his life. For that, and other atchievements, he, when very young, received from the generals crowns and other presents, as the rewards of his valour; and, as his reputation daily encreased, the people chose him Curule Ædile, and the priests created him Augur.

Not long after the first *Punic* war, which had lasted twenty-two years, *Rome* became involved in a war with the *Gauls*; in which the *Insubrians*, who inhabited that part of *Italy* which borders on the *Alps*, applied to their neighbours for assistance, particularly to the *Gesatæ*, who used to hire themselves out for pay. The *Romans* esteemed themselves happy, that they were not engaged in this *Gallic* war before that against the *Carthaginians* was concluded; but that all that time the *Gauls* continued quiet, as if they waited to take up the conqueror. The pro-

---

* Private challenges were unknown to the *Romans*; these were introduced long after in the barbarous ages, and sprung from that gross superstition, which supposed, that the innocent was always the conqueror. The challenges here mentioned, therefore relate to those which frequently passed between the brave men on each side in armies at war, particularly in time of battle.

digious

digious preparations made by the *Romans* on this occasion, as well as their extraordinary sacrifices, evidently shewed the strength of their apprehensions; for, in obedience to some prophecies contained in the books of the *Sibyls*, they buried alive in the place called the Beast-market, two *Greeks*, a man and a woman, and also two *Gauls*, one of each sex *; and these sacrifices gave rise to certain private mysterious ceremonies that still continue to be annually observed in *November*.

Though the *Romans*, in the beginning of this war, sometimes gained very signal victories, they were as often shamefully defeated; but neither their good nor ill success put a final period to the war, till C. *Quintius Flaminius*, and P. *Furius Philo* being consuls, marched with a powerful army against the *Insubrians*. A report then prevailed, that the river, which runs through the country of *Picenum*, was turned into blood; and that, at the same time, three moons were seen at *Ariminum*: besides, the augurs, at the time of chusing the consuls, declared, that the election of those two were unduly and in-

---

* This cruel kind of superstition, practised by a nation esteemed most polite, cannot fail of shocking every humane mind. But, when once men entertain the idea, that the Sovereign of the whole earth delights in the miseries of his creatures, they stop at nothing, and even murder becomes sanctified by the venerable name of religion.

auspiciously made. Upon this the senate instantly dispatched letters to forbid the consuls to act, and to enjoin them to return speedily to *Rome*, in order to resign their office: but *Flaminius* deferred opening these letters, till he had not only fought and defeated the enemy, but ravaged their whole country; after which he returned to *Rome*. But, tho' he brought prodigious spoils, none of the people went out to meet him; nay, he had like to have been denied the honour of a triumph, for not instantly obeying the senate; and the triumph was no sooner ended, than both he and his colleague were deprived of their office, and reduced to the condition of private citizens.

Flaminius and his colleague being thus deposed from the consulate, *Marcellus* was elected in their room, who no sooner entered upon his office, than he chose *Cneius Cornelius* for his colleague. Mean while the *Gauls* sent ambassadors with proposals of peace, which was at last concluded, though the people, at the instigation of *Marcellus*, were desirous of war. However, thirty thousand of the *Gessetæ* soon after passing the *Alps*, joined the *Insubrians*, who were still more numerous, and relying on their numbers, boldly marched as far as *Acerræ*, a city situated between the *Alps* and the *Po*. From thence king *Viridomarus*, at the head of ten thousand of the *Gesatæ*, ravaged the country near that river.

Marcellus receiving an account of their march, left his colleague before *Acerræ*, with a third

third part of the horse, and all the heavy-arm'd infantry, and taking with him 600 of the light infantry, with the rest of the horse, pursued the 10,000 *Gesatæ* without intermission, night and day, till he came up with them near *Clastidium*, a small town in *Gaul*, that had lately been brought under subjection to the *Romans*. He had not time either to refresh his troops, or give them rest; for the Barbarians being soon informed of his arrival, and seeing the small number of his foot, marched directly against him, with *Viridomarus* at their head, uttering dreadful menaces. As *Marcellus* had but few troops, he endeavoured to prevent their being encompassed by the enemy, by extending the cavalry on the wings, till his front was nearly equal to that of the enemy. But, as he was advancing to the charge, his horse, frighted at the shouts of the *Gauls*, suddenly turned short, and, in spite of all his endeavours, carried him back. *Marcellus*, fearing that this might be taken for an ill omen, took his horse by the bridle, and turned him quite round, then returning to his former station, adored the sun; to make them imagine, that his wheeling about was an act of devotion, it being customary with the *Romans* to turn round when they worshipped the gods. He then made a vow to consecrate to *Jupiter Feretrius* the belt of the arms that should be taken from the enemy. At that instant the king of the *Gauls* seeing him, and guessing from the ensigns of authority, that he was the *Roman* general, advanced, brandishing

dishing his spear, and loudly challenging him to the combat. He was of a superior stature to the rest of the *Gauls*, and wore a suit of armour adorned with gold and silver, and variegated with the most lively colours. *Marcellus* immediately calling his eyes on this splendid armour, concluded it was that he had vowed to *Jupiter*, and riding with all his force against *Viridomarus*, pierced his breastplate with his spear, and threw him to the ground, when repeating his blows, he killed him: then leaping from his horse, he stripped him, and lifting the splendid armour towards heaven, cried, " O *Jupiter Feretrius!* who
" from on high, beholdest on the day of
" battle, the brave exploits of captains and
" commanders, I call thee to witness that I
" am the third *Roman* general that has slain
" a general and a king. To thee I conse-
" crate these first and most excellent of the
" spoils: be thou propitious, and in the
" prosecution of this war, crown our actions
" with the like success."

Having finished his prayer, the *Roman* horse began the charge, by attacking both the enemy's horse and foot at the same time, and obtained a compleat victory. Never before or since did such a small body of horse give such an entire defeat to such a superior force both of horse and foot, as were then drawn up against them. *Marcellus* having slain the greatest part of the enemy, and taken all their arms and baggage, marched back to join his colleague, who had not such success in

his

MARCELLUS having kill'd the King of the Gauls, consecrates his spoils to Jupiter Feretrius.

his investing *Milan* *, a very large city, well inhabited, and the capital of all that country: for the *Gauls* defended it with the utmost resolution; but when *Marcellus* returned, the *Gesatæ* finding that their king was slain, and his army defeated, they hastily withdrew. Thus *Milan* was taken, and the *Gauls* delivered up their other cities to the *Romans*, who consented to a peace on reasonable conditions.

It was decreed by the senate, that *Marcellus* should alone have the honour of a triumph; which, from the richness and quantity of the spoils, the great stature of the captives, and its pomp and magnificence, was one of the most splendid that had ever been seen. But the most singular and agreeable sight was *Marcellus* himself; who had caused a branch of a large oak to be cut, on which was fastened the armour of the vanquished Barbarian, disposed in the natural order.

---

* *Acerræ* being taken by *Scipio*, the *Gauls* retired to *Milan*, and were followed by *Scipio*; but, in his return back, the *Gauls* fell on his rear, which they cut to pieces, and routed part of his army; but *Scipio*, having stopped the fugitives, wrested the victory out of the hands of the *Gauls*, and marched back to *Milan*. This is still a very considerable city; of which the reader may see an entertaining description in the ingenious Mr. *Addison*'s *Travels* inserted in *The World Display'd*, vol. xix. pag. 53—60.

When the procession began to move, he ascended his triumphal chariot, and passed through the city, bearing this trophy on his shoulders. The army closed the procession in bright armour, singing songs of triumph, and in praise of *Jupiter* and *Marcellus*, who, on his arriving at the temple of *Jupiter Feretrius*, there fixed and dedicated his trophy.

This victory, and the conclusion of the war, gave such joy to the *Roman* people, that, as a testimony of their gratitude, they caused a golden cup to be made and presented to *Apollo* at *Delphi*; they likewise divided a great part of the spoils among the confederate cities that had sided with them, and also sent considerable presents to their friend and ally *Hiero* king of *Syracuse*.

Afterwards *Hannibal* making an irruption into *Italy*, *Marcellus* was sent with a fleet to *Sicily*. Two years after happened the defeat at *Cannæ*, in which fell many thousands of the *Romans*; and the few who escaped retired to *Canusium*. It was then apprehended, that *Hannibal* would have marched with his victorious army to *Rome*; upon which *Marcellus* sent fifteen hundred of his men by sea to guard the city; and having, by order of the senate, repaired to *Canusium*, he put himself at the head of the troops that had retired to that city after the battle.

By this time war had carried off the chief of the *Roman* nobility, and most of their commanders. Indeed there was still left *Fabius Maxi-*

Maximus *, who was distinguished by his great capacity: but his extraordinary precaution made the *Romans* consider him as a person proper to provide for their defence, but by no means fit to attack an enemy; and therefore applied themselves to *Marcellus*, and that his daring courage might be tempered with the caution of *Fabius*, they often chose them consuls together, and sometimes sent them against the enemy, one as consul, and the other as proconsul. Hence, according to *Posidonius*, *Fabius* was called the *Buckler*, and *Marcellus* the *Sword* of the *Roman* state.

As after the victory, *Hannibal's* soldiers grew careless, and often straggled about in parties in search of plunder, *Marcellus* frequently fell upon them, and thus by little and little diminished the forces of the enemy. He afterwards marched to the relief of *Naples*, and having confirmed the *Neapolitans* in the favourable opinion they had entertained of the *Romans*, entered *Nola*, where the senate were unable to restrain the people, who had embraced the interest of *Hannibal*. In the city was a person named *Bandius*, famed for his personal valour and noble birth, who had distinguished himself at the battle of *Cannæ*, where, after having slain a great number of *Carthaginians*, he was at last found lying covered with wounds on a heap of dead bodies. When *Hannibal* admiring his cou-

---

* See the life of *Fabius Maximus*, where many of these events are related more at large.

rage,

rage, conceived a friendship for him, and not only dismissed him without any ransom, but loaded him with presents. Hence *Bandius*, influenced by gratitude, zealously espoused *Hannibal*'s interest, and endeavoured to bring over the people to join the *Carthaginians*. *Marcellus* thought it would be cruel and dishonourable to put to death a man who had so often exposed his life in fighting for the *Romans*; and who had such humanity and sweetness of temper, that he could hardly fail of gaining the affections of every great and generous mind. One day *Bandius* coming to see him, he pretended as if he did not know him, and asked him who he was. *Bandius* told him his name; when *Marcellus* appearing surprised, and highly pleased, cried, "How! art thou the *Bandius* so much talked "of at *Rome* for his bravery at the battle of "*Cannæ*, who was so far from deserting "*Paulus Æmilius* the conful, that he receiv-"ed into his body several arrows aimed at "that general?" *Bandius* owning himself to be the very person, shewed his scars. "Why "then, returned *Marcellus*, since thou hast "given us so many proofs of thy friendship, "didst thou not come to me at my first arri-"val? Doest thou think I can be ungrate-"ful to a friend who is honoured even by "his enemies?" He then embraced him, and gave him a fine horse, and five hundred drachmas in silver. Thus he bound *Bandius* to him; who, from thence forward, appeared

zealous

zealous in discovering the designs of the party he had before espoused. That party was indeed very numerous, and had laid the design of plundering the baggage and waggons of the *Romans*, as soon as they left the city to engage *Hannibal*. *Marcellus* being informed of this conspiracy, drew up his army in order of battle within the city, and placing his baggage near the gates, forbad the inhabitants appearing on the walls. *Hannibal* now seeing the walls abandoned, imagined there was a great sedition in the city, and from this opinion marched up to it with the less order and precaution. At that instant, *Marcellus* commanding the gate opposite to him to be opened, issued out with the best of the horse, and charged the enemy in front. A second gate was soon after opened, through which the infantry poured with loud shouts. When *Hannibal* attempting to divide his troops, in order to make head against these last, a third gate was opened, out of which issued all the rest of the *Roman* forces. *Hannibal* surprized and disconcerted at this unexpected sally, suffered his troops to be thrown into confusion, and this was the first time in which his forces fled before the *Roman* legions; for they were driven back to their camp in great consternation, and with prodigious slaughter, *Hannibal* losing above five thousand men, and the *Romans* not more than five hundred.

On

On the death of one of the consuls *, the people recalled *Marcellus*, and, in spite of the magistrates, caused the election to be deferred till his return. On his arrival, he was immediately chosen consul; but it happening at that time to thunder, the augurs, though they perceived that this invalidated the election, did not dare to oppose it for fear of the people: *Marcellus*, however, voluntarily laid down his office; on which, being immediately elected proconsul, he returned with the army to *Nola*, where he chastised all who, during his absence, had declared for the *Car-*

---

* *Lucius Posthumius Albinus*, the consul here mentioned, was slain, with his whole army, by the *Gauls*, after a very extraordinary manner. *Livy* says, that he being obliged to pass through the *Litanean* forest, the *Gauls* had cut all the trees near the road in such a manner that they still continued standing, though they might be thrown down with the least motion. *Albinus* being arrived in the forest with his army, consisting of twenty-five thousand men, the *Gauls*, who lay concealed, set the trees near them in motion, which falling on those next them, and they on the next, and so on, they all fell almost at the same time, overwhelming and killing both men and horses. Those who escaped this snare, were killed by the *Gauls*, among whom was the consul himself, whose head they cut off, and emptying his skull, set it in gold, to be used for libations at their feasts.

thaginians

thaginians; on which *Hannibal* hasted to their assistance, and offered him battle, which he refused. But, a few days after, *Hannibal* having sent the greatest part of his army to forage, he attacked him with great vigour, having first furnished his foot with long spears like those used on ship-board, and taught them to wound the enemy with them at a distance; while the *Carthaginians* fought only with short swords, or with darts, which they were unskilled in throwing. Hence, all who attempted to make head against them, fled in confusion, leaving five thousand slain in the field of battle; four elephants were also killed, and two taken alive. Besides, what appeared still of greater consequence, the third day after the battle, above three hundred of the *Spanish* and *Numidian* cavalry deserted to *Marcellus*; a misfortune which *Hannibal* had never before suffered; for, notwithstanding his army was composed of many barbarous nations, as different in their manners as in their languages, he had hitherto preserved among them a good understanding and strict concord. These deserters always continued faithful to the *Romans*.

At length, *Marcellus* being a third time created consul, passed into *Sicily*[*]: for the *Carthaginians* had entertained thoughts of reconquering that island. The city of *Syracuse* had been thrown into confusion by the

---

[*] In the 212th year before the Christian æra.

death of the tyrant *Hieronymus*, and an army had been already sent thither by the *Romans*, under the command of *Appius Claudius*.

Of the *Romans* who had fought at the battle of *Cannæ*, some had fled, and others were taken prisoners; but, though the latter were very numerous, yet, when *Hannibal* offered to release them, for an inconsiderable ransom, their countrymen not only refused it; but giving themselves no farther trouble about them, left them to be killed by the enemy, or sold out of *Italy*; while they transported into *Sicily* those who had escaped by flight, and prohibited their return home till the war with *Hannibal* was ended. *Marcellus* had no sooner arrived in *Sicily*, and taken upon him the command of the army, than great numbers of these unfortunate men came to him, and falling on their knees, besought him with the deepest lamentations and floods of tears, to admit them among his troops, promising to shew by their future behaviour, that their defeat had been owing to some misfortune, and not to cowardice. *Marcellus* being filled with compassion for these exiles, wrote to the senate, to desire leave to recruit his troops out of these men, as he should have occasion; but, after long deliberations, they returned for answer,
" That the *Romans* did not stand in need of
" the assistance of cowards; however, if
" *Marcellus* pleased, he might make use of
" them, provided he did not bestow on them
" crowns,

"crowns, any of the customary rewards of
"valour." This decree gave *Marcellus* great
concern, and at his return to *Rome*, at the
conclusion of the war, he complained, that
after all his services, they had refused him
the pleasure of retrieving the honour, and al-
leviating the misfortunes of his fellow-citizens.

Marcellus, after his landing in *Sicily*, first
endeavoured to be revenged on *Hippocrates*,
the *Syracusan* general; who, to shew his regard to the *Carthaginians*, and by their means
to render himself tyrant of *Sicily*, attacked
the *Romans*, and slew great numbers of them
near *Leontium*. *Marcellus* therefore marching
to that city with his whole army, took it by
storm; but offered no injury to the inhabitants; however, he caused the deserters he
found there to be scourged with rods, and
then put to death. Upon which *Hippocrates*
sent to inform the *Syracusans*, that *Marcellus*
had put to the sword all capable of bearing
arms, and while the inhabitants of *Syracuse*
were in the utmost consternation at this news,
he came and surprized the city.

The *Roman* general now marching with his
whole army, encamped near *Syracuse*, and
immediately sent ambassadors thither, to let
the inhabitants know the whole truth of what
had happened at *Leontium*; but finding that
the *Syracusans*, being awed by the power
of *Hippocrates*, refused to listen to him, he
made preparations for attacking the city both
by sea and land. The land forces were commanded

manded by *Appius Claudius*, while *Marcellus* with sixty gallies, each of which had five rows of oars, attacked it by sea; he had likewise a terrible machine carried on eight gallies fastened together, and was inspired with great hopes by the number of his batteries, the greatness of his preparations, and his own reputation. But *Archimedes* despised all his machines and preparations, which were nothing when compared with the engines he daily invented.

This *Archimedes* had long before been sollicited by king *Hiero*, his friend and kinsman, to reduce his geometrical speculations into practice. One day discoursing on the laws of mechanics, *Archimedes* made use of this proposition, that with any given force the greatest weight might be moved; and added, that if there were another earth besides this we inhabit, by going upon that he could move this. The king surprized at this discourse desired him to prove the truth of his proposition, by moving some great weight with a small force. On which *Archimedes* caused one of the king's gallies to be drawn on shore by the assistance of a great number of men, and then to be filled with its usual burthen and a number of people. This being done, he made use of a machine he had before prepared, consisting of a variety of ropes and pullies, and by only moving the end of this machine, drew the vessel to him as smoothly as if it had floated in the water. At which the king being astonished, and fully convinced of the amazing

amazing power of his art, entreated him to form several kinds of military engines both offensive and defensive. This task he performed; but the greatest part of that prince's reign being free from war, they had never been used; but were all ready on this occasion, and the great artist himself was at hand to direct them.

However, the *Romans* now preparing to storm the walls of *Syracuse* in two places at once, silence and consternation reigned throughout the city, the frighted inhabitants thinking it impossible to resist such numerous forces, and so furious an assault. But *Archimedes* no sooner began to play his engines, than they darted forth against the land forces such a shower of missive weapons, and stones of a prodigious weight, with an amazing noise, and irresistible force and rapidity, that nothing was able to stand before them: they overthrew and destroyed whatever came in their way, and caused a terrible disorder in the ranks of the *Romans*. On the side next the sea were vast machines, which suddenly projected huge beams over the walls, and beating with prodigious force on the *Roman* ships sunk them to the bottom. Others being hoisted up by the prows with iron hooks or claws, were set an end on the stern, and then also plunged to the bottom of the sea. Others again were drawn towards the shore with hooks and cords, and after being whirled about, were dashed to pieces against the rocks that projected out below the walls; and often might

might be seen ships raised a great height above the water, and swinging in the air; thus the men were shaken out, and the vessels either shattered to pieces against the walls, or suddenly let fall, and plunged under water. As to the vast machine brought by *Marcellus* upon eight gallies, *Archimedes* discharged at it, before it came near the walls, a vast piece of a rock, and afterwards a second and a third, by which repeated blows it was shattered and disjointed.

Upon this ill success *Marcellus* retired with his gallies as fast as possible, and at the same time sent orders to the forces on land to retreat. Then calling a council of war, it was resolved to come the next morning before it was light, if possible, close under the walls; for they imagined that *Archimedes*'s engines, being designed to act at a considerable distance, would throw all the stones and weapons over their heads, and thus by their being so near, would have no effect.

But when the *Romans* were close to the walls, and imagined they were by that means skreened from the enemy, they found themselves suddenly attacked on all sides with a shower of darts, and all kinds of missile weapons, and with a multitude of great stones falling perpendicular on their heads. Thus they were soon obliged to retire; and they were no sooner got at a little distance, than they were overtaken by a fresh shower of all sorts of weapons, so that a very great slaughter was made, and many of their
gallies

gallies bruifed, and dafhed in pieces, while the *Romans* were unable to do the leaft damage, or to make the fmalleft impreffion on the works of the enemy: For as moft of *Archimedes*'s machines were concealed by the walls, the *Romans* fuftaining fuch infinite mifchief, without being able to fee from whence it came, feemed to fight againft the gods. *Marcellus* himfelf however efcaped, and, laughing at his own engineers, afked, " Shall
" we continue to fight againft this mechani-
" cal *Briarius*, who, as if in fport, toffes
" our fhips out of the fea, and again plunges
" them into it; and who, for the number
" of the weapons he difcharges againft us,
" even furpaffes what is faid in fabulous ftory
" of the giants with an hundred hands?"
Indeed the *Syracufans* were only as the body of thefe machines, while *Archimedes* was the foul that put them in motion; for all other weapons lay unemployed; and his were the only offenfive and defenfive arms of the city. In fhort, the *Romans* were feized with fuch terror, that if they only faw a fmall cord, or piece of wood about the walls, they inftantly fled, crying, " *Archimedes* is going to
" employ fome terrible engine againft us."

Marcellus obferving this, gave up all thoughts of taking the city by ftorm, and therefore leaving *Appius* with two thirds of the army before *Syracufe*, marched with the reft to befiege *Megara*. Soon after he had taken it, he forced the camp of *Hippocrates*, at *Acrillæ*, and flew 8000 of his men. He then

then over-ran a great Part of *Sicily*, retook many places that had submitted to the *Carthaginians*, and fought several battles, in all which he was constantly victorious.

Afterwards, on his return to the siege of *Syracuse*, he took *Damippus*, a *Spartan*, as he was going from thence by sea; when the *Syracusans* being very desirous of ransoming him, *Marcellus* had several conferences with them on that subject; during which he had an opportunity of observing a tower, which his troops might privately enter, it being carelessly guarded, and the wall that led to it easy to be scaled. Having therefore prepared his scaling-ladders, he executed his design at a time when the *Syracusans* were, with much mirth and jollity, celebrating a feast to *Diana*; so that before it was light, he, without being perceived by the citizens, not only took possession of the tower, but filled the adjoining walls with soldiers, and by force entered the *Hexapylum*. This was no sooner perceived by the *Syracusans*, than they were seen moving about in great confusion; but soon all the trumpets of the *Romans* sounding at once, they were filled with consternation, and fled, imagining that the enemy were in possession of the whole city. But the best and strongest part of it, called the *Achradina* was not yet taken, it being divided by walls from the rest of the city.

This enterprise being executed with such success, *Marcellus* at length entered from the *Hexapylum* into the city, where all his officers fur-

surrounded him, to congratulate him on his success; but viewing from the rising ground, on which he stood, this great and magnificent place, it is said that he wept, from his commiserating the calamity that hung over it; his imagination representing the sad and dismal scene that was approaching, when it should be sacked by his soldiers, who peremptorily demanded leave to plunder it, which none of the officers dared to deny them. Nay, many insisted that the city ought to be burnt, and laid level with the ground; but to this *Marcellus* would not consent; it was with great reluctance that he permitted the riches of the city, and the slaves to become the prey of the soldiers; and he gave strict orders, that no violence should be offered to the person of any freeman, or any citizen reduced to slavery. But notwithstanding his express commands, the city was so severely treated, that he could not help expressing his concern at seeing all its grandeur and felicity vanish in a moment: for the plunder and spoils were said to be as valuable as those that were soon after taken at *Carthage:* for it was not long before all the other parts of the city were taken by treachery, and plundered; the royal treasure was alone preserved, in order to be deposited in the public treasury at *Rome*.

But nothing, on this occasion, gave *Marcellus* such concern as the unhappy fate of the great *Archimedes*, who happened at that time to be so deeply engaged in study, and to have his mind, as well as his eyes, so intent on some geometrical figures, that, not attending to the noise and hurry occasioned by the *Romans*, he did not even know that the city was taken: but while he was thus employed, a soldier suddenly entered his room, and ordered him to follow him to *Marcellus*; which he refusing to do, till he had demonstrated his problem, the fellow was so exasperated, that he drew his sword, and killed him. Others say, that *Archimedes* seeing a soldier coming with a drawn sword to murder him, intreated him to stay a moment, that he might not leave his problem unfinished, and his demonstration imperfect; but that the soldier slew him immediately, without paying the least regard to his request. Others again assert, that as *Archimedes* was carrying some mathematical instruments in a box to *Marcellus*, he was met by some soldiers, who, believing there was gold in it, killed him. All historians however agree, that *Marcellus* was greatly concerned at his death; that he would not even look upon the murderer, whom he detested as an execrable villain; and that, after a diligent enquiry, having found his relations, he loaded them with many signal favours.

Though the *Romans* had hitherto given other nations evident proofs of their courage and military conduct, they had yet shewn them no remarkable examples of humanity and clemency: but *Marcellus* on this occasion shewed the *Greeks*, that the *Romans*

sur-

surpassed them in justice, as much as in valour and conduct: for such was his candour and condescension, that if any thing severe or cruel was committed in the cities he conquered in *Sicily*, the blame might be more justly charged on the sufferers themselves, than on him. I shall only give one instance, out of many, that might be mentioned.

In *Sicily* is a city called *Enguium*, which, though not large, is very ancient, and particularly celebrated for the appearance of the goddesses termed the *Mothers*. As this city favoured the interest of the *Carthaginians*, *Nicias*, the most eminent of the citizens, used his utmost endeavours, by his speeches in all the public assemblies, to make them declare for the *Romans*, on which some of the inhabitants, fearing his great power and reputation, resolved to seize him, and deliver him up to the *Carthaginians*. But *Nicias* discovering their design, thus prevented their putting it in execution. He uttered several disrespectful things of the goddesses, and even represented their appearance in that city as a fable. His enemies now rejoiced at finding, that he himself had furnished them with reasons sufficient to justify whatever treatment they should give him. The day being come on which they had agreed to seize him, there happened to be an assembly of the people, in which *Nicias* made a speech on some affair then under deliberation: but suddenly, in the midst of his discourse, he fell down, and having lain for some time, as if in a trance,

lifted

lifted up his head, and began to speak in a feeble, trembling voice, which he raised by degrees; when, perceiving that the whole assembly, struck with horror, remained in silent consternation, he arose, threw off his mantle, and, tearing his coat in pieces, ran half naked, crying, that he was pursued by the avenging furies; and a kind of religious fear preventing any one's stopping him, he reached one of the city gates without opposition. Mean while his wife, who was in the secret, taking her children in her arms, ran and prostrated herself before the altar of the goddesses; then, pretending to go in search of her husband, who was wandering about the fields, got safely out of the city; and thus both escaped to *Marcellus* at *Syracuse*. Some days after that general entering *Enguium*, loaded the inhabitants with irons, in order to punish them for their insolence and treachery. But *Nicias* falling on his knees before him, with tears in his eyes, asked pardon for all the citizens, and, in the first place, for his enemies. Upon which *Marcellus* relenting, ordered them all to be set at liberty, and forbid the soldiers committing any disorders in the city: he then bestowed on *Nicias* a large tract of land, and many rich presents.

Marcellus being at length recalled by the *Romans*, to conduct a war nearer home, took with him the finest statues, paintings, and furniture in *Syracuse*, in order to adorn his triumph, and to be preserved as lasting ornaments

ments of the city, for *Rome* was yet entirely unacquainted with the elegant works of art: instead of which, were to be seen arms taken from the Barbarians, spoils stained with blood, and triumphal ornaments and trophies that had an unpleasing, and even dreadful appearance. Thus *Marcellus* became the favourite of the people, on account of his embellishing the city, and exposing to their view all the various elegant performances of the *Grecian* artists. The graver citizens, however, preferred *Fabius Maximus*, who, on his taking *Tarentum*, left the pictures and statues of the gods, and took nothing from thence but gold, silver, and other useful riches. These charged *Marcellus* with rendering *Rome* odious, by his leading not only men, but even the gods in triumph; and with spoiling a people inured to husbandry and war, and entirely unacquainted with luxury and sloth, by furnishing them with a pretence for idleness and vain discourse: but notwithstanding these censures, *Marcellus* gloried in being the first who taught the *Romans* to admire, and set a value on the arts of *Greece*.

As *Marcellus* now found that his enemies opposed his being allowed the honour of a triumph, he was contented with celebrating it on the *Alban* mount, and entering the city in that sort of triumph, which the *Romans* term an Ovation. Those to whom this was allowed, did not ride in a triumphal chariot drawn by four horses a-breast, neither were they

they crowned with laurel, nor were preceded by trumpets sounding before them, but went on foot, in slippers, with flutes playing before the conqueror, whose head was crowned with myrtle; which was a sight that carried no appearance of war, and was rather delightful than terrible.

Marcellus being now chosen consul a fourth time, some *Syracusans*, by the persuasion of his enemies came to *Rome* to accuse him before the senate of several unjust and cruel actions, contrary to the league that subsisted between them and the *Romans*. On the day of the arrival of the *Syracusan* deputies, *Marcellus* happened to be offering sacrifice in the capitol: but going directly to the senate, who were then sitting, they fell on their knees, beseeching them to hear their complaints, and to do them justice: on which the other consul, who was present, reproved them for preferring their petition during the absence of his colleague. *Marcellus*, on hearing what was in agitation, hasted to the senate, where, taking his place, he dispatched the ordinary affairs of his office, and then, rising from his seat, went, as a private man, to the place appointed for the accused to make their defence, giving the *Syracusans* full liberty to make good this charge. They were at first struck, and confounded at his unconcern, and the dignity of his appearance; but being animated and encouraged by his enemies, they made their accusation in a speech filled with lamentations and complaints,

plaints, the substance of which was, *That though they were the friends and allies of the Romans, Marcellus had made them suffer what other generals seldom inflict on a conquered enemy.* To which Marcellus answered, *That notwithstanding all the injury they had done the Romans, they had suffered no more than what is impossible to prevent, when a city is taken by storm. That their being so taken, was their own fault, as they had rejected the reasonable proposals which had been offered them; and that they could not pretend that they had been forced by the tyrants to take arms, as they had voluntarily submitted to these tyrants, in order to make war.* The reasons being at length heard on both sides, the deputies were, as usual, ordered to withdraw; as did also *Marcellus*, who left his colleague to take the votes of the senators, while he himself patiently waited at the door till the cause was decided, without shewing the least sign either of concern for the event, or of resentment against the *Syracusans*. At length judgment being pronounced in favour of *Marcellus*, the *Syracusans*, struck with fear, prostrated themselves at his feet, beseeching him to lay aside all resentment, and to pardon not only them, but their fellow-citizens, who would for ever retain a grateful remembrance of that favour. On which *Marcellus*, being moved by their intreaties, had the generosity to forgive them, and from that time did the *Syracusans* all the good offices in his power. In return, the *Syracusans* decreed *Marcellus* all imaginable honours, and even made a law, that whenever he, or any of his family, came to *Sicily*, the *Syracusans* should offer sacrifice to the gods, with chaplets on their heads.

Since the battle of *Cannæ*, the other consuls and generals had taken all possible measures to avoid coming to a battle with the *Carthaginians*. But *Marcellus* being now sent against *Hannibal*, took a quite contrary course, from the persuasion that delay, which, was thought the best method of ruining *Hannibal*, would also destroy *Italy*: for he thought *Fabius** was like an unskilful physician, who, from fear, defers giving his patient strong, but efficacious medicines, till his spirits become exhausted, and nature sinks beyond the possibility of a recovery. He first retook the principal cities of the *Samnites*, which had revolted from the *Romans*, and found in them not only great quantities of corn and money, but 3000 soldiers left by *Hannibal* for the defence of those cities, whom he made prisoners. Afterwards *Cneius Fulvius*, the proconsul, with eleven tribunes, being slain, and the *Roman* army defeated in *Apulia*, *Marcellus* sent letters to *Rome*, to animate the people, by assuring them, that he was on his march against *Hannibal*, and would soon lessen the joy he felt for his late success. But we are told by *Livy*, that these letters only served to increase their fears; they feeling greater

---

* See the life of *Fabius Maximus*, in Vol. II.

pain

pain from their present danger, than for their past loss, on account of their esteeming *Marcellus* a greater general than *Fulvius*.

Marcellus, now marching into *Lucania*, found the enemy encamped on inaccessible mountains, on which he himself encamped in the plain, and the next day ranged his army in order of battle; when *Hannibal* coming down, a very bloody engagement ensued, which began at the third hour, and continued till the two armies were separated by the night; yet the next morning, at break of day, *Marcellus* again drew up his army among the dead bodies on the field of battle, and challenged *Hannibal* to renew the engagement, and decide the contest. But he chusing rather to retire, *Marcellus* caused the spoils of the enemy to be gathered, and the bodies of the dead to be burnt, and then marched in pursuit of him. *Hannibal*, however, laid several ambuscades for him; but he had the address to escape them all, and had, besides, the advantage in every encounter and engagement, which so far increased his reputation at *Rome*, that, on the approach of the time for the election of new consuls, the senate thought it most advisable to recal *Lævinus*, the other consul, from *Sicily*, than to give the least interruption to *Marcellus*, who opposed *Hannibal* with such success. After which, *Quintus Fulvius* was chosen dictator, and *Marcellus* continued in his command under the quality of proconsul.

It being afterwards agreed by letters, that *Fabius Maximus* the conful should besiege *Tarentum*, while he should prevent *Hannibal*'s relieving that place, he marched after him with the utmost expedition, and came up with him at *Canusium*; when *Hannibal*, continually shifting his camp to decline coming to a battle, *Marcellus* pursued him closely, encamped constantly in his sight, and appeared every morning ready to engage him; at last, coming unexpectly upon him, when he was encamping in a plain, he so harrassed his army by little skirmishes, that a general battle at length ensued, which lasted till they were parted by the night: but early the next morning, the *Romans* again appeared in order of battle. This greatly enraged *Hannibal*, who assembling his army, made a speech, in which he exhorted the soldiers to fight with their usual bravery, in order to support the glory they had already gained, and to secure the fruits of their former victories: " For you see, " said he, after all our success, and our be- " ing so lately conquerors, we are scarce al- " lowed time to breathe; nor are we likely " to enjoy the least quiet, till we drive this " man back." Instantly both armies charged with great fury: but at length, *Marcellus* seeing his right wing pressed hard, ordered one of his legions to advance from the rear to the front, which occasioning a disorder among his troops, the *Romans* were defeated, and lost above two thousand men on the spot.

Marcellus

Marcellus then retreated to his camp, and summoning the army before him, told the soldiers, that he saw the arms and bodies of *Romans*, but not one *Roman* among them; and, on their asking his pardon for their fault, he replied, that this they must not expect while they continued beaten, but that it should be granted as soon as they had conquered; and that the next morning he would lead them again to battle, that the news of their victory might reach *Rome* before that of their flight. On his dismissing them, he ordered, that barley instead of wheat should be given to the companies that had turned their backs and lost their colours. The soldiers were so affected by this discourse, that tho' many of them had suffered much, and were deeply wounded, there were none among them who did not feel more pain from his words, than from their wounds.

Early the next morning, the scarlet robe, which was the signal of battle, was hung out, when the companies that fled in the last engagement, at their earnest request, obtained leave to be placed in the foremost rank; and then the rest of the troops were drawn up in their proper order. This being told to *Hannibal*, he cried, "Ye gods! what is to
" be done with a man who is affected neither
" by good nor bad fortune? He alone, when
" conqueror, gives us no rest, and when
" conquered, takes none himself. We must
" resolve to fight with him for ever; for the
" glory of a victory, and the shame of a defeat,

"feat, equally inspire him with new cou-
"rage, and spur him on to fresh attempts."

Both armies soon engaged; when *Hanni-
bal*, seeing the advantage equal on both sides, ordered the elephants to be brought up, and driven against the van of the *Roman* army. These at first occasioned some terror and confusion; but *Flavius*, a tribune, snatching an ensign, boldly advanced, and, with the point of it, wounded the first elephant, which turning back, ran upon the second, and the second upon the third, till they were all thrown into confusion. *Marcellus* perceiving this, resolved to take advantage of the disorder caused by the elephants, and ordering the horse to attack the *Carthaginians*, they did so with great fury, and soon drove them, with prodigious slaughter, back to their intrenchments. In this battle, eight thousand of the enemy were slain, and on the side of the *Romans* three thousand, besides almost all the rest were wounded. This gave *Hannibal* an opportunity of decamping by night, and of removing to a considerable distance; for *Marcellus* was prevented by the number of the wounded from pursuing him; he therefore retired with his army by slow and easy marches into *Campania*, and in order to recover and refresh his soldiers, spent the summer at *Sinuessa*.

Mean while *Hannibal*'s army being under no manner of restraint, ravaged several parts of *Italy* with fire and sword. This
gave

gave occasion to the enemies of *Marcellus* at *Rome* to incite *Publius Bibulus*, one of the tribunes of the people, a man of a violent temper, and a considerable orator, to form an accusation against him. This coming to the ears of *Marcellus*, he committed the care of the army to his lieutenants, and hastened to *Rome* to refute the calumnies uttered by his enemies. On his arrival, he found that a charge was drawn up against him, in which he was accused of having left the seat of war, in order to go to the baths to refresh himself after his fatigues. On the day when his cause was to be tried, *Bibulus* ascended the tribune's seat, and accused him with great vehemence. The answer of *Marcellus* was plain and short, but the great men and principal citizens warmly engaged in his defence, exhorting the people not to shew themselves worse judges than the enemy, by condemning for cowardice the only *Roman* general whom *Hannibal* was sollicitous to avoid, and, in short, *Marcellus* was not only acquitted, but was a fifth time chosen consul.

Marcellus no sooner entered upon his office, than going to the several cities of *Tuscany*, he put a stop to a very dangerous sedition, and at his return, having built a temple out of the spoils brought from *Sicily*, he resolved to dedicate it to *Virtue* and *Honour*; but was prevented by the priests, who would not allow one temple to contain two deities. When being highly displeased at the opposition he had met with, he began to build another to *Virtue*. As several other omens happened at the same time, the augurs still detained him at *Rome*, notwithstanding his extreme impatience to come to a decisive battle with *Hannibal*. However, as soon as the diviners had finished such sacrifices and expiations as they thought proper, *Marcellus* and his colleague departed in order to prosecute the war against the *Carthaginians*, and encamping between the cities of *Bantia* and *Venusia*, endeavoured by all possible means to bring *Hannibal* to a battle, which he, with equal industry, strove to avoid; but being informed that the consuls had sent troops to besiege the city of the *Epizephyrians*, or western *Locrians*, he laid an ambuscade near the hill of *Petilia*, and slew two thousand five hundred *Romans*. This heightening *Marcellus*'s desire of coming to a battle, he encamped nearer to the enemy.

As there was between the two armies a small hill that had a pretty steep ascent, and was covered with bushes and thickets, with holes and ditches on its sides, from whence issued several springs, the *Romans* were surprized that *Hannibal* on coming first to so commodious a place should not have taken possession of it. Though *Hannibal* might think this a proper place for a camp, he judged it much fitter for an ambuscade, and therefore chose to put it to that use, and not doubting that so advantageous a situation would entice the *Romans* thither, filled the

thickets

thickets and hollows with spearmen and archers. Indeed this hill instantly became the subject of conversation in the *Roman* camp, and, as if all the soldiers had been generals, every one expatiated on the advantages they should obtain by encamping, or at least raising a fortification, on this hill. *Marcellus* therefore resolved to take a view of the place himself, and took with him *Crispinus* his colleague, his son *Marcellus*, who was a tribune, and about two hundred and twenty horse, all *Tuscans*, except forty *Fregellanians*, who had given him signal proofs of their fidelity, affection, and courage. On the summit of the hill, which was woody, and covered with brambles, was placed a centinel, who seeing, without being discovered, all the motions of the *Romans*, gave intelligence of every thing that passed to those who lay in ambush: these therefore lay close, till finding that *Marcellus* had reached the foot of the hill, they suddenly rushed out, and having discharged a shower of arrows, attacked him on all sides with their swords and spears, some rushing on those who stood their ground, and others pursuing those that fled. The *Tuscans* having run away at the first charge, the forty *Fregellanians* closed together in a body, in order to defend and save the consuls: but at length *Crispinus*, being wounded by two arrows, turned his horse to make his escape; and *Marcellus* being run through the body with a lance, fell down dead; then the few remaining *Fregellanians* made their escape,

and

and carrying off the son of *Marcellus*, who was wounded, fled with him to the camp. In this skirmish, the number of the slain did not amount to much above forty; and only eighteen were taken prisoners, besides five lictors: but *Crispinus* died a few days after of his wounds*.

The *Romans* had never before the misfortune to lose both their consuls in one engagement. *Hannibal*, who at first imagined this defeat of little consequence, no sooner heard that *Marcellus* was slain, than he hasted to the place of battle, and on his approaching the body, stood for some time to view it, without uttering one insulting word, or discovering the least sign of joy at the death of so formidable an enemy. But appearing surprized at the strange and undeserved death of so great a man, took the signet from *Marcellus*'s finger, and gave orders that his body should be magnificently adorned and burnt; which being performed, he caused his ashes to be put into a silver urn covered with a crown of gold, and sent them to his son. But some *Numidians* meeting those who carried the urn, attacked them in order to seize it; and, while the others stood on their defence to preserve it, the ashes in the scuffle happened to be spilt; which being told to *Hannibal*, he cried, " It " is impossible to oppose the will of the " gods." He however punished those *Nu-*

---

* This skirmish, so fatal to *Marcellus*, happened in the 206th year before the birth of our Saviour.

HANNIBAL concerned at seeing the dead Body of MARCELLUS his Enemy.

midians: but took no care to collect the ashes, imagining, that the gods had decreed that *Marcellus* should die after so strange a manner, and his remains be denied the honour of a burial. These particulars are mentioned by *Valerius Maximus* and *Cornelius Nepos*; but *Livy* and *Augustus Cæsar* say, that the urn was actually carried to his son *Marcellus*, and honoured with a magnificent funeral.

The public donations of *Marcellus*, besides what he dedicated at *Rome*, were a magnificent *Gymnasium*, which he built at *Catana* in *Sicily*, and several pictures and statues brought from *Syracuse*, which he set up in the temple of *Minerva* at *Lindus*, in which was also a statue of himself; and, in the temple of the gods called *Cabiri* in the island of *Samothracia*. His family flourished with great splendor till the reign of *Augustus*, when *Marcellus* died very young, soon after he had married *Julia*, that emperor's daughter. To his honour *Octavia*, his mother, dedicated a library, and *Augustus* a theatre, which were named the library and theatre of *Marcellus*.

We have now given the most remarkable circumstances in the lives of *Pelopidas* and *Marcellus*, whence it appears, that both were endowed with magnanimity and courage, indefatigable industry, and uncommon strength of body: but *Marcellus* suffered great slaughter to be committed in most of the cities he stormed; while, to the honour of *Pelopidas* and *Epaminondas*, they never spilt the blood

commander the world had ever seen; that *Pyrrhus* was the second, and himself the third: on which *Scipio* asked him with a smile, "What would you have said had you vanquished me?" "*Scipio*, he replied, I would not then have reckoned myself the the third, but the first commander."

The *Romans* recollected, and mentioned with admiration, these instances of *Scipio*'s behaviour, and were the more incensed against *Titus*. There were, however, many who applauded the action; for they considered *Hannibal* as a fire which only wanted bellows to blow it into a flame; and there are some who tell us, that *Titus* did not act thus of his own accord, but was joined in commission with *Lucius Scipio*; and that the whole design of their embassy was to effect the death of that brave *Carthaginian*.

There are no other accounts after this of the life of *Titus*, either in relation to war, or the administration of the government, and we are only informed that he died a natural death.

If we compare *Philopœmen* with *Titus*, we shall find, that neither *Philopœmen*, nor any other man, conferred such benefits on *Greece* as *Titus*; for they were *Grecians* making war on *Grecians*; while *Titus* was a *Roman*, who fighting in their behalf, recovered them from their subjection to the *Macedonians*, and then generously restored their liberties. The former indeed, by the numerous victories he obtained,

obtained, acquired more trophies; while *Titus* decided the contest betwixt himself and *Philip* in two engagements: but *Rome* shared in the glory of the latter, who made use of the forces of that great and flourishing state; while *Philopœmen*'s glory was intirely his own: the one had brave and well-disciplined troops under his command; the other rendered those brave whom he commanded, he being forced to new discipline, and new model his soldiery. Thus what is of the greatest moment in gaining a victory, was the invention of the one, while the other practised only what was already in use. As to acts of personal bravery, there are many of *Philopœmen*'s, but none of *Titus*'s: *Philopœmen* ran with his drawn sword wherever he saw the *Macedonians* standing firm and fighting bravely; but *Titus* stood still, with his arms stretched open, imploring the gods. *Titus*, it is true, acquitted himself well, both as a governor and ambassador; but *Philopœmen* was no less serviceable to the *Achæans* as a private man than as a commander; for whenever the public good required it, he waited not the formality of being chosen general, but conferred the command upon himself, and was chearfully obeyed. In fine, *Titus*'s equity, clemency, and humanity towards the *Grecians*, are proofs of a great and generous mind; but *Philopœmen*'s resolution in asserting the liberty of his country, against the *Romans* whom he suspected, is something still

greater;

greater; as it is a more difficult task to oppose the powerful, than to relieve the distressed. Upon the whole, the preference may be given to the *Roman* with respect to justice and clemency, and to the *Grecian* for bravery and skill in military affairs.

THE

THE LIFE OF PYRRHUS.

ACIDES king of the *Molossians*, had, by his wife *Pthia*, *Pyrrhus*, the subject of this history, and two daughters, *Deidamia* and *Troias*; but being deposed in an insurrection, the *Molossians* raised to the throne one of the sons of *Neoptolemus*, and murdered all the friends of *Æacides* that fell into their hands. *Pyrrhus*, then an infant, was saved by *Androclides* and *Angelas*, who secured him from the assassins, and fled with a few domestics, and some women who were the child's nurses: but these retarding their flight, they were soon overtaken by the enemy. In this extremity, they committed the infant prince to the care of *Menander*, *Hippias*,

numerous, that it would be a labour to reckon them up, was never wounded: but it may be said in excuse for *Pelopidas*, that besides being transported by the heat of battle, his heroic ardour was inflamed by a brave and noble desire of being revenged on a tyrant who was a disgrace to human nature. On the other hand, *Marcellus* was not carried away by the fury and enthusiasm that stifles reason, and shuts the eyes in the greatest danger, but rushed headlong into it, like a scout or spy. I would not be thought to intend this as an accusation against these great men; but rather as a complaint of the injury they did themselves in preferring their courage to all their other virtues, and rashly sacrificing their lives, when they ought to have preserved them for the service of their country, their friends, and their allies. *Pelopidas* was interred by those in whose cause he was slain, and the funeral pile of *Marcellus* was lighted by the very enemies who slew him. The former was an high honour, but the latter was still more glorious, since it is much more for an enemy to admire and reverence the virtue by which he has suffered, than for a friend to be grateful for the benefits he has received.

THE LIFE

OF

ARISTIDES.

THIS great *Athenian* was the son of *Lysimachus*, and is said to have been always very poor, while some have taken great pains, tho' with little appearance of truth, to prove that he was rich. He was the intimate friend of *Clisthenes*, who settled the government of *Athens* after the expulsion of the *Pisistratidæ*; and had a particular veneration for the memory of *Lycurgus* the *Spartan* legislator; whence he came to be a favourer of aristocracy, in which he was constantly opposed by *Themistocles*, who was equally zealous for a popular government. According to some authors, they were always at variance when

ARISTIDES.

when boys, even in their sports and diversions; and, it is said, that the difference of their tempers was early discovered by their continual opposition: *Themistocles* being compliant, daring, artful, and subtle, variable, but eager and impetuous in his pursuits; while *Aristides* was firm and steady in his resolutions, immoveably just, and incapable of the least falshood, flattery, disguise, or deceit. *Themistocles*, by gaining friends, obtained considerable interest and authority; and being told that he would govern the *Athenians* admirably, if he would but take care to avoid partiality, he answered, "May I never sit on a tribunal where my friends will not be more respected and favoured than strangers." But *Aristides* would never do the least injustice to oblige his friends; for it was his opinion, that the security of a good citizen, must always consist in doing and advising what is just and fit to be done.

In the mean while *Themistocles* opposing him in all his designs, *Aristides* was reduced to the necessity of obstructing whatever he proposed, as well in his own defence, as to put a stop to his growing power, which, by the favour of the people, was daily encreasing: for he chose to oppose some things that would be of real advantage to the public, rather than to suffer the power of the commonwealth to fall into his hands. Thus when *Themistocles* one day recommended something that would be of great advantage, *Aristides* opposed him warmly, and with succefs; but, on his leaving the assembly, he could not forbear crying aloud, That the *Athenians* would never be safe till they threw *Themistocles* and him into the *Barathrum* *. Thus he frequently proposed his sentiments, by a second or third person, for fear *Themistocles*, from envy or hatred to him, should oppose what would be of public advantage.

Aristides was deservedly admired for his firmness and constancy in the sudden and unexpected changes that frequently happen to persons concerned in the great affairs of state. Being neither elated by honours, nor dejected by disappointments, he enjoyed constant ease and serenity of mind: for it was his fixed opinion, that a man ought to be wholly at his country's command, and on all occasions be ready to serve it, without any of the selfish views of honour and profit; and his propensity to justice was so strong, as not to suffer him to be influenced either by frendship or enmity. Thus, it is said, that when prosecuting one who had injured him, finding, after he had finished his accusation, that the judges were going to pass sentence without hearing the accused, he seconded the request

* This was a deep pit into which condemned prisoners were cast head-long. It was a dark and noisome hole, and had sharp spikes at the top, that none might escape out, and others at the bottom, to pierce those that were thrown into it. *Potter's Antiquities*, vol. i. p. 134.

of his adversary, who desired to be heard, and pleaded that he ought not to be denied the benefit of the laws. Another time, sitting as judge between two private persons, and one of them saying that his adversary had frequently injured *Aristides*, "Friend, said he, "interrupting him, tell me only what injuries he has done to thee, for I set here to judge thy cause, not mine."

On his being chosen public treasurer, he soon shewed, that not only those of his time, but the preceding officers, had applied great part of the public money to their private use, particularly *Themistocles*, who, notwithstanding his wisdom and bravery, took every means of enriching himself. When *Aristides* therefore was to bring in his accounts, *Themistocles* raised a strong party against him, and accusing him of misapplying the public money, procured his condemnation: but the principal persons in the city opposing so unjust a sentence, he was not only freed from the fine imposed on him, but appointed treasurer for the following year. He then rendered himself acceptable to those who robbed the public, by being less strict in examining their accounts; upon which they gave him the highest commendations, and made interest with the people for his being continued another year in his office. But, on the day of election, when the *Athenians* were unanimously going once more to appoint him treasurer, he severely rebuked them. "When I "discharged my office faithfully and with "honour,

"honour, said he, I was reviled and dis-
"graced; but now I have suffered your trea-
"sury to be plundered by these public rob-
"bers, I am applauded as the best of citi-
"zens. But I am more ashamed of the ho-
"nour done me to-day, than of the sentence
"passed against me last year: for with con-
"cern and indignation I see, that you think
"there is greater merit in obliging ill men,
"than in faithfully managing the public re-
"venue." Thus he stopped the mouths of
all who plundered the public, even while
they were extolling him, and giving ample
testimony in his behalf.

The king of *Persia* sending a fleet, on the pretence of taking revenge on the *Athenians* for their burning of *Sardis*, but really to conquer all *Greece:* this fleet no sooner arrived at *Marathon*, than the *Persians* began to ravage all the neighbouring country. Upon this the *Athenians* appointed ten generals to command in that war; the chief of whom was *Miltiades*, and the next to him in authority and reputation was *Aristides*. *Miltiades*, in a council of war, proposing to give the enemy battle, *Aristides* seconded him, and the generals having the chief command by turns, when the day came on which *Aristides* had the command, he resigned it to *Miltiades*. Thus preventing all jealousy and contention, he made the other generals sensible of their happiness, in being guided by a person of the greatest experience, so that, resigning also their turns, and submitting entirely to his orders, *Miltia-*
des

des had the undivided and absolute command of the army. As in this battle the main body of the *Athenian* army was hard pressed, by the Barbarians making their greatest efforts there, *Aristides* and *Themistocles* placed themselves at the head of the tribes to which they belonged, and opposed the enemy with such bravery and resolution, that they were put to flight and driven back to their ships. The *Greeks* then perceiving that the Barbarians, instead of returning towards *Asia*, were forced by the winds and currents towards *Attica*, and fearing that they would surprize the city of *Athens*, when unprovided for a defence, they hasted with nine tribes to its assistance, and marched with such expedition *, that they arrived there the same day.

Aristides was left with his tribe at *Marathon* to guard the prisoners and booty, and fully answered the high opinion that had been entertained of him; for, notwithstanding there being great quantities of gold and silver in the camp, and the tents with the ships they had taken, contained rich apparel, and all kinds of wealth, yet he forbore to touch any thing; but he could not render every one equally honest. For notwithstanding the strictness of his orders, some, unknown to him, obtained great wealth. Among these

---

* The distance from *Marathon* to *Athens* is forty miles.

was *Callias* the torch-bearer †, who being privately met by one of the Barbarians, was perhaps taken by him for a king, on account of the length of his hair, and his head being encompassed by a fillet; for the Barbarian fell on his knees before him, and discovered to him a great quantity of gold hid in the bottom of a well: on which *Callias* had the injustice and cruelty to kill the man on the spot, to prevent his discovering the treasure to others.

Of all the virtues of *Aristides*, that by which he was most distinguished was his justice, which was so eminent, that he acquired the most noble and divine appellation of *The Just*: a title of which kings and tyrants were never fond, they chusing rather to be stiled *Nicanors*, or conquerors; *Cerauni*, thunderbolts; *Poliorcetes*, takers of cities; while others, preferring the brutal power of doing mischief to the divine attribute Virtue, have been pleased with the appellation of *Eagles* and *Vultures*. But, though the surname of *Just* at first procured *Aristides* respect and love, it at last excited envy. This was principally owing to *Themistocles*, who spread a report among the people, that *Aristides*, by making himself sole arbitrator and judge in all disputes, had abolished all courts of judica-

† This was a very confiderable office, as the Torch-bearer was admitted to the most secret mysteries of religion. The villain here mentioned was cousin-german to *Aristides*.

ture,

ARISTIDES.

ture, and infensibly rendered himself supreme, though he had neither guards nor attendants. The people, grown infolent by their late fuccefs, thought that every thing ought to depend on their pleafure, and looked with refentment on every man of fuperior eminence and reputation. They therefore affembling at *Athens* from every part of *Attica*, banifhed *Ariftides* by the oftracifm, difguifing their envy of his glory, under the fpecious pretence of hatred to tyranny. Thus it was ufual for every *Athenian* who envied the growing greatnefs of another, to difcharge all his fpleen and malice by a ten year's banifhment.

The affair of the oftracifm was conducted in the following manner: every citizen took a fhell or a piece of broken pot, and having wrote on it the name of the perfon he would have banifhed, carried it to a certain part of the market-place inclofed with wooden rails. The magiftrates then began to count the number of the fhells, or bits of pot; for, if there were not fix thoufand, the oftracifm was void; but, if the number was compleat, every name was laid by itfelf, and that perfon whofe name was found on the greateft number of pieces was declared banifhed for ten years; but he was allowed to enjoy the produce of his eftate. It is faid that when the citizens were infcribing their names on the fhells, in order to banifh *Ariftides*, an illiterate man came to him, and giving him a fhell, defired him to write *Ariftides* upon it. When being a little

furprized,

surprised, he asked the fellow, if *Aristides* had ever injured him: "No, not in the least, replied the other, I do not so much as know him; but I am weary of hearing him every where called *the Just*." To this *Aristides* made no answer, but, taking the shell, wrote his own name upon it, and returned it to be used against himself. On his leaving the city to go into banishment, he lift up his eyes to heaven, and generously prayed to the gods, *that the* Athenians *might never see the day when they should be forced to remember* Aristides.

When *Xerxes* marched three years after, through *Thessaly* and *Bœotia*, to *Attica*, the *Athenians*, apprehending, that should *Aristides* join the enemy, he might induce many of the citizens to go over to them, they published a decree to call home all the exiles. But they mistook the character of *Aristides*; for he had constantly animated the *Greeks* to maintain their liberty, and after the decree, when *Themistocles* was chosen general, he had the magnanimity to join him, and from the love he felt for his country, generously sacrificed all private resentment, and by assisting him with this person and counsel, contributed as much as was in his power to raise his greatest enemy to the highest pitch of glory[*]. *Themistocles*, struck with the nobleness of soul he discovered in their first inter-

[*] See these particulars more fully related in the life of *Themistocles*, inserted in Vol. I.

ARISTICLES generously offers his assistance to THEMISTOCLES his Enemy.

ARISTIDES.

view, confessed, that he was ashamed in being thus excelled in generosity, and, laying open his secret designs, *Aristides* readily assisted him in executing them. While the *Grecian* commanders were debating, whether they should comply with the desire of *Themistocles*, who had bravely resolved to attack the *Persian* fleet, *Aristides* perceiving that *Psyttalia*, a small island in the streights, opposite to *Salamin*, was in the possession of the enemy, he landed with some of the bravest and most resolute of his countrymen, and attacking the enemy with the utmost intrepidity, they were all cut to pieces, except some of the principal persons, who were made prisoners; among whom were three sons of *Sandauce*, the sister of *Xerxes*, whom *Aristides* instantly sent to *Themistocles*, and it is said, that, at the command of a certain oracle, they were, by the direction of *Euphrantides*, the diviner, sacrificed to *Bacchus*. As the heat of the battle was round *Psyttalia*, *Aristides* placed troops on its coast, that none of the friends of the *Athenians* might perish, nor none of their enemies escape; and after the battle was over, a trophy was erected in that island.

Themistocles had no sooner defeated the *Persian* fleet, than he proposed to *Aristides*, their breaking down the bridge that *Xerxes* had formed over the *Hellespont*. This *Aristides* warmly opposed, lest it should force the *Persians* to make an obstinate defence. *Themistocles* therefore sent one of the captives privately

vately to inform the king, that, from his desire to serve him, he had used his utmost endeavours to divert the *Greeks* from this design of destroying the bridge over the *Hellespont*. At which *Xerxes* being alarmed, retired with the utmost expedition, but left behind him an army composed of 3,000,000 of his best troops.

This prodigious army kept up the fears of the *Greeks*, while their apprehensions were increased by the haughty letters they received from the king's lieutenant-general, who, in one of them, said, " You have defeated at " sea men unskilled at the oar, and only ac" customed to fight on land; but the plains " of *Thessaly* and *Bœotia* afford us an opportu" nity of letting you see the bravery of our " horse and foot." But, in his letters to the *Athenians*, he offered to rebuild their city, to give them large sums of money, and to render them the masters of *Greece*, on condition of their withdrawing their forces, and giving their allies no farther assistance. The *Lacedæmonians*, fearing these proposals would be accepted, sent ambassadors to intreat the *Athenians* to send their wives and children to *Sparta*, for their greater security; and with offers of supporting likewise the old and infirm; for *Athens* having been destroyed, and the country ravaged by the *Persians*, the people suffered the extremest poverty. But the *Athenians*, by the advice of *Aristides*, returned the ambassadors this noble answer; *That they forgave their enemies, for thinking that every thing*

thing was to be purchased by money, because they, perhaps, knew nothing of greater value; while they were highly offended, that the Lacedæmonians, regarding only their present poverty and distress, and, forgetful of the honour and virtue of the Athenians, should think an allowance of bread to their poor, the only sufficient motive to induce them to continue firm to their alliance, and to fight for the safety of Greece. The ambassadors having received this answer, *Aristides* ordered them to tell the *Lacedæmonians*, That all the gold upon earth, and all contained within its bowels, was less valuable to the Athenians, than the liberty of Greece. Then the ambassadors from the *Persians* being called in, *Aristides*, shewing them the sun, said, That so long as that luminary continued its course, so long would the Athenians wage war against the Persians, to revenge the burning of their temples, and the plundering of their country. He also preferred a decree, that whoever should send ambassadors to the *Persians*, or desert the *Grecian* alliance, should be solemnly cursed by the priests.

Mardonius, the lieutenant-general of *Xerxes*, soon after making a second incursion into *Attica*, the *Athenians* again retired to the isle of *Salamin*. Mean while, according to *Idomeneus*, *Aristides* was sent ambassador to *Sparta*, where he reproached the *Lacedæmonians* with their abandoning *Athens* again to the Barbarians, and earnestly exhorted them to march speedily to the relief of that part of *Greece* which was not yet fallen into the

hands

hands of the enemy. The Ephori, however, seemed but little moved with this exhortation, and it happening to be the festival of *Hyacinthus*, they spent the whole day in feasting and merriment; but at night privately difpatched 5000 *Spartans*, each taking with him feven *Helots*. Afterwards, *Ariſtides* complaining again, the Ephori told him with a fmile, that he muſt either doat or dream, fince their army had by that time advanced as far as *Oreſtium*; to which *Ariſtides* replied, that it was not then a time to divert themfelves, by deceiving their friends inſtead of their enemies. However, in *Ariſtides*'s decree, no mention is made of his being fent, the ambaſſadors being *Cimon*, *Xanthippus* and *Myronides*.

Some time after, *Ariſtides* being appointed commander in chief of the *Athenian* forces, he marched with 8000 foot to *Plataea*, where he was joined by *Pauſanias*, general of all *Greece*, at the head of the *Spartans*, and the other *Grecian* troops daily arrived in great numbers. The *Perſian* army, which was encamped along the fide of the river *Aſopus*, covered a prodigious tract of ground, in the middle of which was thrown up a fquare wall, ten furlongs in length, on each fide, for the fecurity of their baggage and valuable effects.

Ariſtides fending to confult the oracle of *Apollo* at *Delphi*, was anfwered, That the *Athenians* fhould gain the victory, provided they offered their fupplications to *Jupiter*, to

Juno

ARISTIDES.

Juno the patroneſs of mount *Citheron*, to *Pan*, and to the nymphs *Sphragitides*,* ; and alſo ſacrificed to ſeveral heroes that were mentioned, and fought only in their own country in the plain of *Ceres*, the *Eleuſinian*, and *Proſerpine*. At this anſwer *Ariſtides* was much perplexed, for if they fought in the plain of the *Eleuſinian Ceres*, the ſeat of war muſt be transferred into *Attica*. Mean while *Arimneſtus*, the *Plataean* general, dreamed that *Jupiter*, the Saviour, coming to him, aſked, What was the reſolution taken by the *Grecians?* to which he anſwered, We ſhall march to-morrow, to engage the enemy, according to the directions of the oracle, into the territories of *Eleuſis*. To which the God replied, that, upon enquiry, he would find, that the place mentioned by the oracle, was the country round *Plataea*. *Arimneſtus* no ſooner awoke, than, ſending for the moſt aged of his countrymen, he, by conſulting them, at laſt found, that at the foot of mount *Citheron*, was a very old ſtructure called the temple of *Eleuſinian Ceres* and *Proſerpine*, and conducting *Ariſtides* to the place, they found it very proper for drawing up an army of foot not well provided with horſe ; after which the *Plataeans*, in order that the oracle might be obeyed in every particular, made a decree to alter the boundaries between their country and *Greece*, by enlarging the

* The nymphs of mount *Citheron* were thus called.

territories of *Attica*, that, according to the direction of the oracle, the *Athenians* might engage the enemy in their own dominions.

It being soon after proposed to draw up the whole army in order of battle, a warm dispute arose between the *Tegeatæ* and the *Athenians*; the former pretending, that, as in all battles, the *Lacedæmonians* commanded the right wing, so the honour of commanding the left was due to them; and in justification of this pretension, they alledged the memorable exploits of their ancestors. As this highly exasperated the *Athenians*, *Aristides* advanced into the midst of them, and said, "This is not a proper time to dispute with "the *Tegeatæ* about their valour and brave "exploits; we shall content ourselves with "telling you, O *Spartans!* and all the "other *Grecians*, that it is not the post that "gives or takes away courage, and that "whatever post you shall assign us, we will "strive to render it honourable, by behaving "in such a manner, as to reflect no disgrace "on our former atchievements. We are come "not to contend with our friends, but to "fight with our enemies; not to boast of "our ancestors, but to exert our bravery in the defence of *Greece*". On hearing this, the council of war declared in favour of the *Athenians*, and gave them the command of the left wing.

Afterwards *Mardonius* being desirous of trying the courage of the *Grecians*, sent his cavalry, in which his principal strength consisted, fifted, to fkirmifh with them. All the *Greeks* were encamped in ftrong and ftony places, at the foot of mount *Citheron*, except the *Megarenfians* who amounted to 3000, and were in the plain. The *Perfian* horfe therefore attacking them on every fide, they were unable to oppofe the fuperior power of the enemy, and fent to *Paufanias* for affiftance. When that general perceiving the camp of the *Megarenfians*, darkened by the clouds of darts thrown into it by the Barbarians, was at a lofs how to act; and feeing no poffibility of repulfing the enemy with his heavy armed *Spartans*, endeavoured to awaken the emulation of the commanders about him, that, from a point of honour, they might eagerly undertake the defence of the *Megarenfians*. When *Ariftides*, perceiving that they all declined it, gave orders to *Olympiodorus*, the braveft of all his officers, who had under his command a body of 300 men, and fome archers. Thefe were ready in an inftant, and with the utmoft expedition marched againft the Barbarians. *Mafiftius*, general of the *Perfian* cavalry, who was diftinguifhed by his ftrength and graceful mien, no fooner faw them, than he advanced to meet them, and a fharp conteft enfued, in which *Mafiftius*'s horfe being wounded by an arrow, threw his rider, who was hindered by the weight of his armour from rifing, and yet could not be eafily flain, tho' the *Athenians*, who thronged about him, affaulted him on every fide; for he was entirely covered with

with gold, brass, and iron: but the vizor of his helmet leaving part of his face unguarded, an *Athenian* ran his pike into his eye, and slew him; upon which the *Persians* left his body, and fled. There were but a small number of the *Persians* slain in the field of battle; but they were so afflicted for the death of *Masistius*, that they cut off their hair, with that of their horses and mules, and filled the air with their cries, he being the next person in the army for courage and authority to *Mardonius*.

Both armies after this continued long inactive; the diviners, who examined the intrails of the sacrifices, equally assuring the *Greeks* and *Persians* of victory, on condition of their remaining on the defensive. At length, however, *Mardonius* finding that his provisions would last only a few days, and that the *Grecian* forces were continually encreasing, by the daily arrival of fresh troops, resolved to wait no longer, but to pass the *Asopus* the next morning, at break of day, in order to attack the *Greeks*, whom he expected to find unprepared. But at midnight a horseman arriving at the *Grecian* camp, desired the centinels to call *Aristides*, when that general coming immediately, he cried, " I " am *Alexander*, king of *Macedon*, who, from " my friendship for you have exposed my- " self to the greatest dangers, to prevent " your being so surprized by a sudden at- " tack, as not to exert your usual bravery " and resolution. *Mardonius*, having a scar-
" city

"city of provisions, is resolved to give you
"battle to-morrow, tho' the augurs endea-
"vour to divert him from it, and his sol-
"diers are fearful and desponding; but he
"is forced to run the hazard of a battle,
"since, by delaying it, he would see his
"whole army perish for want." *Alexander* then desired *Aristides* to remember him as his friend, and not to reveal this intelligence to any other person. *Aristides* shewed the necessity of mentioning it to *Pausanias*, who was general in chief; and the king of *Macedon* returning to his camp, he immediately went to *Pausanias*'s tent, and told him what he had heard.

Upon this news all the officers were sent for, and ordered to prepare for battle. *Pausanias*, at the same time, told *Aristides*, that he proposed to remove the *Athenians* from the left wing to the right, that they might be opposite to the *Persians*, against whom they would fight with the greater bravery, from their having already experienced their manner of combat, and their being animated by their former success; while he intended to command the left wing, where he should be obliged to fight the *Greeks*, who had embraced the *Persian* interest. The other *Athenian* officers were greatly offended, that *Pausanias* should thus take upon him to remove them, as if they were slaves, at his pleasure. But *Aristides* addressing them, said, "It is
"but a few days since you disputed with the
"*Tegeatæ* for the command of the left wing,
"and

"and having gained it, considered it as a
"great honour; and now the *Spartans* are
"willing to give you the command of the
"right wing, you are displeased at the ad-
"ditional honour, and insensible of the ad-
"vantage of not being obliged to fight
"against your countrymen, but only against
"Barbarians, who are naturally your enemies."

Inspired by these words, the *Athenians* readily changed posts with the *Spartans*, and exhorted each other to exert themselves with the utmost bravery. "The enemy have
"neither better arms, nor bolder hearts,
"said they, than they had at *Marathon*;
"they have the same bows, the same orna-
"ments of gold; the same embroidered
"habits; the same soft and effeminate bodies.
"While we have still the same arms, with a
"courage heightened by our victories: nor
"do we, like them, fight for cities and
"tracts of land; but for the trophies of
"*Salamin* and *Marathon*." But *Mardonius* being informed of this change, either from his fear of the *Athenians*, or his resolution to engage the *Spartans*, placed the *Persians* in his right wing, and the *Greeks* of his party in his left, opposite to the *Athenians*. Upon this *Pausanias* also changed again, and returned to the right wing; *Mardonius* still followed his example, posting himself in the left, that he might be opposite to the *Spartans*, and thus the day passed without coming to a battle.

In the evening a council of war was held in which it was resolved to decamp: the springs near the camp being disturbed and
spoiled

spoiled by the enemy's horse. At night the officers begun to march at the head of their troops, to a place marked out for a new camp, but the soldiers following unwillingly, were no sooner out of their intrenchments, than the greatest part of them made towards the city of *Plataea*, and some running one way, and some another, pitched their tents as they pleased, without order or discipline. Mean while a party of the *Lacedaemonians*, under the command of *Amompharetus*, staid behind, he declaring that this decampment was a disgraceful flight, and protesting, that, instead of deserting his post, he would still remain there with his troops, and receive and sustain the whole force of the enemy. *Pausanias* having in vain represented to him, that he ought to submit to the resolution taken by the *Greeks* in council, sent to desire the *Athenians*, who were before, to halt, that they might all proceed in a body, and at the same time marched, with the rest of the army, towards *Plataea*, hoping that *Amompharetus* would by that means be induced to quit his post, and join him, as he really did.

Day by this time beginning to appear, *Mardonius*, who had been informed of the decampment of the *Grecians*, marched against the *Lacedaemonians*, in order of battle, the Barbarian soldiers shouting, as if they were sure of destroying and plundering them in their flight. *Pausanias*, on perceiving this motion, stopped, and ordered every one to his post; but great part of the army still continued irregularly scattered in small parties,

ties, even after the fight began. In the mean time he offered sacrifice, but finding no propitious omens, ordered the *Lacedæmonians* to lay their shields at their feet, and without opposing the enemy attend his orders. He then offered another sacrifice; mean while, the enemy's horse were still advancing, and coming within reach, some of the *Spartans* were wounded with arrows, and among others, *Callicrates*, the tallest and most comely person in the whole army. That brave officer being ready to expire, said, That he did not lament his death, since he came from home, with the design of sacrificing his life for the safety of *Greece*; but was sorry to die without having once drawn his sword against the enemy. The steadiness and bravery of the *Spartan* army, while in this situation, were worthy of the highest admiration; for making no defence against the enemy who charged them, but expecting the signal from the gods and the general, they patiently suffered themselves to be wounded and slain in their ranks.

Pausanias being deeply concerned at seeing the priests offer one sacrifice after another, without obtaining one favourable omen, suddenly turned with his eyes full of tears, to the temple of *Juno*, and, lifting up his hands, besought that goddess, the patroness of *Citheron*, and the other tutelar deities of the *Platæans*, that, if the fates had not decreed that the *Grecians* should prove victorious, they might be at least allowed to sell their lives dearly, and not perish without
shewing

shewing the enemy, that they were to contend with men of bravery and experience. On his finishing this prayer, the sacrifices appeared propitious, and the diviners assured him of victory. The orders were given, and in an instant the *Spartan* battalions appeared like the single body of some fierce animal, erecting his bristles, and preparing for combat. The Barbarians now saw, that they were to fight with men who were determined to conquer or die; therefore, covering themselves with their targets, they discharged their arrows against the *Spartans*, who, moving in a close compact body, attacked them, forced their targets out of their hands, and directed their blows at the faces and breasts of the *Persians*; but many of the latter, after their being thrown down, broke the *Lacedæmonian* spears with their hands, and then rising, betook themselves to their swords and battle-axes.

Mean while the *Athenians* waited in expectation of being joined by the *Lacedæmonians*; but being informed by an officer dispatched to them by *Pausanias*, that the battle was begun, hastily marched to their assistance; but were met by the *Grecians* who had sided with the enemy. *Aristides*, on seeing them, advanced before his army, and, calling aloud, conjured them by all the gods of *Greece*, to cease that impious war, and not oppose the *Athenians*, who were marching to the assistance of those who were hazarding their lives for the safety of *Greece*; but perceiving

ceiving that no regard was paid to his words, and that they march'd to oppose him, he attacked them, tho' they amounted to near 50,000 men. This engagement was hottest against the *Thebans*, the most powerful of whom having sided with the *Persians*, had by their authority brought out the *Theban* troops contrary to their inclinations.

Thus was the battle divided into two parts. The *Lacedæmonians* first broke and routed the *Persians*, *Mardonius* himself being slain by a blow on the head with a stone, after which they pursued the Barbarians to their camp, which was encompassed, and fortified with wood. Soon after the *Athenians* routed the *Thebans*, killing 300 of the most considerable persons among them on the spot. Just as they began to give way, news was brought, that the Barbarians were shut up and besieged by the *Lacedæmonians*; upon which the *Athenians* giving the *Greeks* an opportunity to escape, marched to join the *Lacedæmonians*, who being unskill'd in sieges made but a small progress in the attack; however, on the arrival of the *Athenians*, the camp was soon stormed, and a prodigious slaughter made of the Barbarians, for of 300,000 men, only 40,000 escaped.

Yet this glorious victory was very near proving fatal to *Greece*; for the *Athenians* absolutely refusing to give up the honour of the day to the *Spartans*, or to permit their erecting a trophy, they were ready to decide the dispute by force of arms; when *Aristides* wisely

ARISTIDES.

wisely interposing, prevailed on them to defer the decision of the affair to the *Grecians*; who being assembled, *Theogiton* the *Megarensian*, observed, that the honour for which they contended, ought to be adjudged to neither *Athens* nor *Sparta*, unless they were resolved to kindle the flames of a civil war. *Cleocritus* the *Corinthian*, then rising, it was imagined he would demand this honour for his own country, *Corinth* being the most considerable city in *Greece*, next to *Athens* and *Sparta*; but they were agreeably surprised, to hear him expatiate in praise of the *Platæans*, and propose, that to extinguish that dangerous contention, they should give the reward and glory of the victory to them. Upon which *Aristides* first agreed to this proposal, in the name of the *Athenians*, and afterwards *Pausanias* for the *Lacedæmonians*.

Thus being reconciled, they presented eighty talents to the *Platæans*, which they employed in erecting a magnificent temple to *Minerva*, and a separate trophy was raised both by the *Athenians* and *Lacedæmonians*. On their sending to consult the oracle of *Delphi*, about the sacrifice to be offered, they were told, that they should erect an altar to *Jupiter the Deliverer*, but forbear sacrificing upon it, till they had extinguished all the fire in the country, on account of its having been profaned by the Barbarians, and that afterwards fire should be brought from the altar of *Delphi*. The *Greeks* were no sooner informed of this, than the generals going all over the country, caused the fires to be extinguished, and *Euchidas* a *Platæan*, promising to bring fire with the utmost speed from the altar of *Apollo*, went to *Delphi*, where having sprinkled and purified himself with water, he placed a crown of laurel on his head, and taking fire from the altar, hasted back to *Platæa*, where he arrived before sun set, performing that day a journey of a thousand furlongs: but he had no sooner saluted his fellow-citizens, and delivered the fire to them, than he fell down and expired; on which the *Platæans* interred him in the temple of *Diana Euclcia*, and erected a tomb to his memory.

At the next general assembly of *Greece*, a decree was proposed by *Aristides*, that a council of deputies from all the *Grecian* cities should be annually held at *Platæa*, and that every fifth year games of liberty should be celebrated: that, by a general levy made over all *Greece*, there should be raised 10,000 foot, 1000 horse, and 100 ships, to carry on the war against the Barbarians; but, that the *Platæans* should be considered as sacred, and be only employed in offering sacrifices to the gods, for the welfare of *Greece*. This decree being passed, the *Platæans* undertook to perform an annual sacrifice in honour of the *Greeks* slain there, which they still perform in the following manner: At day-break, on the 16th day of the month *Maimacterion*, or *November*, the procession begins with a trumpet sounding the signal of battle; then follow

low several chariots filled with garlands, and branches of myrtle: next comes a black bull, after which proceed some young men who are free born, carrying the usual libations, vessels filled with wine and milk, oil and ointments; no slave being allowed to be present at a solemnity performed in honour of those who died in the cause of liberty; and the procession is closed by the archon, or chief magistrate of *Platæa*, clothed in a purple robe, wearing a sword, and carrying in his hand a water-pot. Being arrived at the burying-place, he takes water out of a fountain, washes the small pillars of the monuments, and rubs them with sweet ointments: after which he kills the bull upon a pile of wood. Then having offered his supplications to the * terrestrial *Jupiter* and *Mercury*, he invites the brave men who died in the defence of *Greece* to this funeral banquet, and pouring out a bowl of wine, says, " This I pre- " sent to those who died for the liberty of " *Greece*."

Aristides, on his return to *Athens*, finding that the people, elated by their victories, endeavoured by all possible means to get the government into their hands, and to establish

* By the terrestrial *Jupiter* they meant *Pluto*. The epithet terrestrial was also given to *Mercury*, on account of his conducting souls into the lower regions.

a democracy, propofed a decree, that every citizen fhould have an equal right to the government, and that the archon fhould be chofen out of the whole body of the people, without diftinction.

Being afterwards joined in commiffion with *Cimon*, and fent againft the Barbarians, they both behaved to the troops of the allies with fuch affability and courtefy, that they infenfibly ftole away the fovereign command from the *Lacedæmonians*; for, while the juftice of *Ariftides*, and the candour of *Cimon* endeared the *Athenians* to the confederates, *Paufanias* rendered himfelf hated for his avarice and cruelty; he fpoke to the officers with fternnefs and feverity, and for the fmalleft offence the common foldiers were either whipt, or obliged to ftand a whole day with an anchor on their fhoulders: nor did they dare to provide forage for their horfes, ftraw for themfelves to lie on, or to touch a fpring of water, till the *Spartans* were firft ferved; his fervants being conftantly pofted with whips in their hands, to drive away thofe who approached. The fea captains, and the officers at land, particularly thofe of *Chios*, *Samos*, and *Lefbos*, were fo exafperated at his behaviour, that they preffed *Ariftides* to accept the poft of general in chief of all the confederate forces; and he anfwering, That they ought to perform fome action that would afford a proof of their fincerity, *Uliades* of *Samos*, and *Antagoras* of *Chios*, boldly attacked *Paufanias*'s galley at the head of the whole fleet near *Byzantium*.

On

ARISTIDES.

On which *Paufanias* told them, they should soon see, that it was not his galley, but their own country they had infulted. To which they replied, That the best thing he could do was to retire, and thank *Fortune* for her favours at *Plataea*, since nothing but their regard for that great action reftrained the *Greeks* from revenging the ill treatment they received from him. In fhort, the allies now renounced their fubmiffion to the *Spartans*, and ranged themfelves under the *Athenian* banners. Even the *Spartan* people on this occafion fhewed an uncommon greatnefs of mind; for finding that their generals were corrupted by power and authority, they voluntarily refigned the command of the confederate forces, chufing rather to fee their fellow-citizens prudent, modeft, and careful to preferve their laws and cuftoms, than to enjoy the command of the united forces of all *Greece*.

While the *Lacedæmonians* had the command, the *Grecians* paid a tax * towards carrying

---

* The great reputation *Ariftides* gained by this taxation, was ridiculed by *Themiftocles*, who ufed to fay, that the praife he received on this account, was not that of a man, but of a ftrong box, which fafely keeps the money put into it without diminution. By this fneer he endeavoured to revenge a ftroke of raillery, which had ftung him to the quick. *Themiftocles* faying, that, in his opinion, the greateft excellency a general could poffefs, was his being able

ing on the war; but being now defirous that every city fhould be rated in the moſt equitable manner, they entruſted *Ariſtides* with the care of examining all the lands and revenues, that all might pay according to their ability. Thus *Ariſtides* became in a manner the maſter of *Greece*; but, inſtead of reaping the leaſt perſonal advantage from it, he levied the tax with ſuch difintereſtednefs, tendernefs and humanity, as to render it eafy and agreeable to all: whence the confederate *Greeks*, celebrated this taxation as the ancients did the reign of *Saturn*, calling it *the happy fortune of Greece*.

Though *Ariſtides* raiſed the city of *Athens* to the higheſt pitch of glory, by eſtabliſhing her dominion over fo many people, he himſelf continued poor till his death, eſteeming his poverty as glorious as all the laurels he had obtained. He gave a remarkable proof of his great candour and moderation, in his refuſing to join the enemies of *Themiſtocles* in their accuſations againſt him, and in his being as far from inſulting him, when he was able to foreſee the deſigns of an enemy. "This "excellence, *Ariſtides* replied, is neceſſary; "but there is another no lefs noble and wor- "thy a general, which is to have clean hands, "and a foul fuperior to venality and intereſted "views."

sent into banishment, as he had been from envying him in his prosperity.

Some assert, that *Aristides* ended his life at *Pontus*, whither he was sent to manage some affairs relating to the public; others say, that he died at *Athens* of old age, in great honour, esteem, and veneration with his fellow-citizens: but *Craterus*, the *Macedonian*, gives the following account. *Themistocles*, says he, was no sooner banished, than the pride and insolence of the populous gave rise to many base informers, who attacked the reputation of the best and greatest men in the city. *Aristides* himself did not escape, for being accused by *Diophantus* of *Amphitrope*, of taking a bribe from the *Ionians*, at the time of his levying the tax, he was fined fifty *minæ*, which being unable to pay, he set sail from *Athens*, and died in *Ionia*. But *Craterus* produces no authorities in proof of this; and tho' almost all the other authors who expatiate on the injustice of the *Athenians* towards their governors, mention the banishment of *Themistocles*, the imprisonment of *Miltiades*, and the banishment of *Aristides* by the ostracism, none of them take the least notice of this condemnation. Besides, his monument is still to be seen at *Phalerum*: it was erected at the charge of the city of *Athens*; for he did not leave enough behind him to defray the expences of his funeral. It is also said, that the city gave each of his daughters, at their marriage, 3000 drachmas

out

out of the public treasury, and bestowed on *Lysimachus*, his son, 100 minæ of silver, and a plantation of as many acres of land, besides a pension of four drachmas a day. It is also said, *Lysimachus*, leaving at his death a daughter named *Polycrite*, the people gave her the same allowance as those who conquered at the *Olympic* games.

THE LIFE OF CATO THE CENSOR.

MARCUS *Cato* is said to have been born at *Tusculum*, from which place his family originally came; but that before he interfered in public affairs, he resided at an estate left him by his father, near the country of the *Sabines*. It was usual with the *Romans* to call those who received no dignity from their ancestors, but began to distinguish themselves, by their personal virtues, *New Men*; whence this appellation was bestowed upon *Cato*: but he used to maintain, that tho', with regard to honours and dignities, he

was

was new, yet with respect to the great actions of his ancestors, he was extremely ancient. His first name was *Priscus*, which he afterwards changed to that of *Cato*, which was a name given by the *Romans*, to those they esteemed wise. His hair was red, and his eyes grey; and, by temperance and exercise, he acquired both health and strength. Eloquence he esteemed necessary for every one who would not pass an obscure and inactive life; he therefore took care to cultivate it by pleading in the boroughs and villages, by which means he at length acquired the reputation of being a good orator: from that time he discovered a gravity of behaviour, a greatness of mind, and a superiority of genius, that shewed him fit for the management of the most important affairs; but tho' he made his disinterestedness and contempt of money appear by his pleading in defence of all who applied to him, without any fee, yet his principal ambition was not to shine at the bar, but in the army, by distinguishing himself in the field.

When very young, his breast was covered with scars from the wounds he had received in battle: for he was only seventeen years of age at the time of his making his first campaign, when all *Italy* was ravaged by *Hannibal*. He always stood firm, struck with great strength, looked fierce at the enemy, and spoke to him in a stern voice, and with threatning language; and he often observed, that such behaviour frequently strikes more

terror

terror than the sword itself. He constantly marched on foot, carrying his own arms, followed by one servant, who was loaded with his provisions: and with him, it is said, he was never angry, whatever food he provided for him; but when he was at leisure from military duty, he would assist him in dressing it. During the whole time of his being in the army, he drank only water, unless when he was extremely thirsty, he would ask for vinegar*, or when fatigued and dispirited, he would drink a little wine.

Near his country-house was a little farm, which had formerly belonged to *Marius Carius*, who had been thrice honoured with a triumph. *Cato* frequently walked thither, and reflecting on the small piece of land belonging to it, and the meanness of the dwelling, used to consider, that he who was once the greatest man in *Rome*, who had conquered the most warlike nations, and even expelled *Pyrrhus* out of *Italy*, had with his own hands cultivated that little spot, and after so many triumphs, dwelt in so poor a cottage. That there the ambassadors of the *Samnites* found him dressing turnips in his chimney corner, and offering him as a present a great quantity of gold; he answered, *That he who could be content with such a supper, wanted no gold, and that, in his opinion, it was more glorious*

* All the *Roman* soldiers carried vinegar with them, to correct the water they were obliged to drink, which was sometimes very bad.

to conquer those to whom it belonged, than to possess the gold itself. *Cato* thought there was true greatness of soul in this simplicity, and, making it his model, encreased his daily labour, and retrenched all his unnecessary expences.

Cato, when very young, served under *Fabius Maximus*, when he took the city of *Tarentum*, and happening to lodge with *Nearchus*, a *Pythagorean*, was desirous of hearing some of his philosophy, on which reasoning, like *Plato*, he told him, that pleasure is the greatest evil; and that the soul being encumbered by the body, could only disengage itself by such thoughts as separate it from all corporeal passions and affections; he was so charmed at this discourse, that he became more in love with temperance and frugality. It is said, that he learned *Greek* very late, and did not begin to read the *Grecian* authors till he was advanced in years; but among these he received considerable advantage from *Demosthenes*, in improving his eloquence. Indeed his writings are enriched with histories and maxims borrowed from the *Greeks*.

Valerius Flaccus, a man of great power and eminence, who loved to encourage rising merit, having an estate adjoining to *Cato*'s, frequently overheard his servants talk of his neighbour's industry and temperance; that he went early in the morning to the neighbouring villages, to plead and defend the causes of those who applied to him; and,

Cato at Dinner with VALERIUS Flaccus, who from thence forward becomes his Friend.

returning to the field, laboured with his domestics, in summer naked, and in winter with only a mean jacket over his shoulders; and when they had all done their work, sat with them at the same table, eat of the same bread, and drank of the same wine: they also repeated many of his sayings, which were full of wit and good sense. Pleased with these accounts, *Valerius* sent to invite him to dinner; and soon discovered, that he possessed such sweetness of temper, such probity and good sense, that, thinking him an excellent plant that deserved to be removed into a better soil, he persuaded him to go to *Rome*, and apply himself to the affairs of the government.

At *Rome*, he, by his pleadings, gained many friends and admirers, and was first made military tribune, and afterwards quæstor. Having acquired great reputation in these posts, he was joined with *Valerius* in the office of consul, and afterwards in that of censor. Among all the ancient senators, he chiefly attached himself to *Fabius Maximus*, whose character and manner of life he esteemed the best model, by which to form his own; he therefore made no scruple of differing with the great *Scipio*, who, tho' very young, was one of those who most opposed the power of *Fabius*. Being sent quæstor with *Scipio*, in the *African* war, and finding that he lived in *Sicily*, at a very great expence, and even without the least œconomy distributed mo-
'ney

ney among his troops, he remonstrated to him, that the greatness of the expence was the least part of the damage, since it was an irreparable injury, thus to corrupt the ancient simplicity of the soldiers life, and accustom them to luxury, by allowing them more pay than was necessary for their subsistence. *Scipio* replied, that a Treasurer was unnecessary in a war carried on with such expedition, and that he was obliged to give the people an account of his exploits, but not of the money he spent. Upon this *Cato* returned to *Rome*, where *Fabius* and he loudly exclaimed in the senate, That *Scipio* trifled away his time in theatres and places of exercise, as if instead of being sent to make war, he was only gone to exhibit games, and public diversions. Tribunes were therefore sent to *Sicily* to examine into the affair, with orders to bring back *Scipio* to *Rome*, if the accusation proved true. But on their arriving in the army, *Scipio* represented, that the success of the war entirely depended on the great preparations made for it; and that when at leisure, he had lived chearfully among his friends, but that his liberality had not prevented his observing the strictest discipline, or his amusements rendered him remiss in the management of important affairs. Satisfied with this answer, the tribunes permitted *Scipio* to set sail for *Africa*.

The power and reputation which *Cato* acquired by his eloquence daily encreasing, he was generally stiled the *Roman Demosthenes*.

In

In eloquence, however, he had many rivals; but it was very extraordinary to meet with persons, who, like him, would copy the example of their forefathers by enduring bodily labour, and be satisfied with frugal meals, a plain dress, and a poor cottage, accounting it more honourable to want, than to possess superfluities. No longer was the state able to preserve the severity of its ancient discipline, on account of its vast extent, and the numerous nations, who submitting to its government, introduced a variety of new customs and modes of life. Justly therefore was *Cato* admired, who, when the people were softened by pleasure, wore, as he himself says, a cheap garment, and even when he was consul, drank the same wine with the servants, while the provisions for his table at dinner never cost above thirty asses *. This he says was done from love to his country, that his body being rendered strong and robust by a plain spare diet, might be more able to endure the fatigues of war. He adds, that in all his country houses, he had not a wall plaistered or white-washed †; that he never gave more than 1500 drachmas for a slave, refusing those that were handsome

---

* About 1 s. sterling.
† The simplicity of life, which consisted in abstaining from the most innocent, and the most elegant enjoyments, however it might be
admired

some and genteel, and chusing only such as were strong and fit for labour, and these he sold when they grew old, that he might not be obliged to maintain them when grown useless.

According to some, this conduct proceeded from the most sordid avarice; while others maintain, that he acted thus in order to correct, by his example, the extravagance and luxury of his fellow-citizens. I cannot, however, help considering it as a sign of a mean and ungenerous spirit, to treat servants like beasts of burthen, and to turn them off, or to sell them, when they have spent their strength, and are grown old in our service, as if sordid interest was the only bond that bound man to man. This is a conduct entirely inconsistent with justice and humanity. Good-nature, which has even a more extensive sway than the laws of mere equity, should not only be extended to man, but to the very brutes that have served us: acts of kindness

admired by the ancients, was not always laudable. There is indeed the truest wisdom and the greatest glory, in preferring an honest poverty, to the splendor that can only be purchased by vice: but when this was not the case, it could only proceed from avarice, or a want of taste, which is generally attended with barbarity of manners. *Plutarch* justly censures *Cato*'s conduct with respect to his slaves, as both inhuman and unjust.

and beneficence will flow from a good and generous mind, like water from an exuberant fountain; and a man of humanity will take care of his horses and dogs, not only while they are young and useful, but even when old, and past their labour. Thus, after the *Athenians* had finished the temple called *Hecatompedon*, they set at liberty the beasts of burthen who had been employed in that work, suffering them to feed at large, and exempting them from all farther service. For creatures, endued with life, ought not to be used as we do our shoes, or our furniture, which we throw away when worn out with use; on the contrary, we should habituate ourselves to tenderness and compassion in the lowest instances, in order to learn benevolence to mankind. As for myself, I would never sell an ox who had laboured till he was grown old in my service; much less could I bear, for the sake of a little money, to part with an old servant, and to expel him, as it were, from his country, by turning him out of my house, and obliging him to quit his usual place of abode and manner of life, especially as he would be as useless to the purchaser, as he was to me the seller.

However, *Cato*'s frugality with respect to the public money, was very extraordinary. While he was governor of *Sardinia*, though his predecessors used to put the public to great expence for tents, for bedding and clothes, for a numerous retinue of friends and domesticks, and for plays and entertainments,

ments, he appeared with the utmoſt plainneſs, and on his viſiting the cities under his government, went on foot, attended only by one public officer, who carried his garment, and a veſſel for ſacrificing: but though this pleaſed all under his command, he made them feel his authority, by being inexorable with reſpect to public juſtice, and inflexibly rigid in the execution of all his orders; ſo that never before did the *Roman* government appear to that people at once ſo terrible and ſo amiable.

His ſtile reſembled his conduct and behaviour; it was facetious and familiar, and yet grave, nervous, and ſententious. And as *Plato*, ſpeaking of *Socrates*, ſays, " That to " ſtrangers he appeared an ignorant rude " buffoon; but within was full of virtue, " and ſpoke ſuch pathetic and divine things " as would move the very ſoul, and force " tears from the eyes of the hearers;" the ſame may be ſaid of *Cato*: he uſed to ſay, *That he had rather do well, and not be rewarded, than do ill, and not be puniſhed; and that he could pardon the faults of other men, but never forgive his own.* Being deſired by *Scipio* to favour thoſe who had been baniſhed out of *Achæa*; when the affair came before the ſenate, great debates aroſe, ſome ſpeaking for the return of the exiles, while it was oppoſed by others: but *Cato* riſing up, ſaid, *We trifle here a whole day, as if we had nothing elſe to do but to debate, whether a number of old Grecians ſhall be interred by our grave-diggers, or*
by

by their own. He frequently said, *That he never repented but of three things, that he had trusted a secret to a woman; that he had gone by water when he might have gone by land; and that he had spent a day without doing any thing:* and to a debauched old man he said, *Friend, old age has deformities enough of its own; do not therefore add to it the deformities of vice.*

On his being chosen consul with his friend *Valerius Flaccus,* the government of *Spain Citerior* fell to his lot; where, after having subdued some of those nations by force of arms, and won over others by kindness, he was suddenly encompassed by an army of Barbarians, and in danger of being driven out of his new settlements; upon which he immediately sent to desire the assistance of his neighbours the *Celtiberians:* but they insisting on being paid 200 talents as a reward for their service, his officers exclaimed, that it was intolerable that the *Romans* should be obliged to purchase the assistance of Barbarians. *Cato* answered, *This agreement is not so bad as you imagine; for, if we conquer, we will pay them at the enemy's expence, and, if we are conquered, there will be no body either to pay or to make the demand.* He however obtained the victory, and afterwards every thing succeeded according to his wishes. *Polybius* observes, that the walls of all the cities of *Spain* on this side the *Batis,* were, by his order, demolished in one day, though they were very numerous; and *Cato* himself says, that he took more cities than he spent days in his

expe-

expedition: this indeed was true; for their number amounted to 400.

Though his troops took in this war a prodigious booty, he besides gave to every soldier a pound of silver, observing, *It was better that all should return home with a little silver, than only a few with a great deal of gold.* He himself assures us, that during the whole war, nothing came to his share, but what he eat and drank. *Not*, said he, *that I blame those who make an advantage of these opportunities; but I had rather contend with the best men for valour, than with the richest for wealth.*

While *Cato* was employed in settling the affairs of *Spain*, *Scipio* being desirous of the honour of finishing the war, prevailed so far by his interest, as to be chosen to succeed him in that government, and then made all possible haste to take the command of the army from *Cato*; who hearing of his march, went to meet him with 500 horse, and five companies of foot, and by the way defeated the *Lacetanians*, and taking among the prisoners 600 *Roman* deserters, had the cruelty to cause them all to be put to death. Mean while the senate decreeing that nothing established by *Cato* should be altered, the post *Scipio* had obtained rather lessened his glory than *Cato*'s, the time of his government being spent in profound peace.

Cato soon after attended the consul *Tiberius Sempronius* in his expeditions into *Thrace*, and
to

to the *Danube*, as his lieutenant; and afterwards he served as a tribune under the consul *Manlius Acilius Glabrio*, who was sent into *Greece* against *Antiochus*, who seemed, next to *Hannibal*, the most formidable enemy f the *Romans*; for, after he had taken from *Seleucus Nicanor* all his provinces in *Asia*, and conquered several barbarous but warlike nations, he turned his victorious arms against the *Romans*, under the specious pretence of delivering the *Grecians*, though they were already restored to liberty by the *Romans*, who had freed them from the *Macedonian* yoke.

The *Grecians*, corrupted by the great hopes given them by their orators, whom *Antiochus* had gained over to his interest, were unresolved how to act; but *Acilius* sending ambassadors to them, confirmed them in their duty; *Titus Flaminius* also easily baffled the attempts of those orators, and *Cato* had equal success with the people of *Corinth*, *Ægium*, and *Patræ*; he likewise staid a long time at *Athens*.

Mean while *Antiochus*, having taken possession of the Streights of *Thermopylæ*, and added to the natural strength of the place both walls and entrenchments, thought himself secure from being attacked by the *Romans*, while they despaired of being ever able to force those passes. But *Cato* recollecting, that the *Persians*, by taking a circuit, had formerly attacked the *Greeks*, began to march by night with part of the army. While they were endeavouring to reach the summit of a

moun-

mountain, the guide, who was a prisoner, lost his way, and wandering among impassable places and precipices, filled the soldiers with the utmost dread and terror. When *Cato* perceiving their danger, ordered the rest of the army to halt, and taking with him *Lucius Manlius*, who was extremely expert in climbing the steepest mountains, he with great pains and danger, marched forwards in a very dark night, clambering among wild olive trees, up steep and craggy rocks, that stopped their view, and prevented their seeing before them. At length, after inconceivable pains, they found a small path, that seemed to lead to the foot of the mountain, where the enemy were encamped. Upon this they set up marks on some of the most conspicuous rocks, and returning back, brought the army by the direction of the marks they had left to the path, where they halted, and made a proper disposition of the troops. But on their advancing a little farther, they had the mortification to find, that the path suddenly failed them, and they perceived before them a steep precipice, which again reduced them to despair: but soon the day beginning to appear one of them thought he heard a noise, and a little after perceived the *Grecian* camp, and their advanced guard at the foot of the rock. *Cato* therefore halting, gave orders that the *Firmians* should come to him: these troops had, on several hazardous occasions, given him signal proofs of their courage and fidelity; and now encompassing him,

he

CATO THE CENSOR.

he told them, that he wanted to take one of the enemy alive; on which they instantly rush'd down the mountain, and attacking unexpectedly the advanced guard, threw them into disorder, dispersed them, and taking one prisoner, brought him to *Cato*; who learning from the prisoner, that the main body of the army was encamped with the king in the narrow passes; and that the detachment that guarded the eminences amounted to 600 select *Ætolians*, drew his sword, and marched against them with loud shouts and the sound of trumpets. When the *Ætolians* perceiving them pouring down from the mountains, fled precipitately to their main guard. At the same time *Manlius*, with the body of the army, forced *Antiochus*'s intrenchments below; and, in this attack *Antiochus* being wounded in the mouth by a stone which beat out his teeth, the pain he felt obliged him to retire; and, as after his retreat, no part of his army dared to stand the shock of the *Romans*, they were entirely routed; when notwithstanding they had no hopes of escaping, on account of the narrowness of the road, and the deep marshes and rocky precipices with which it was surrounded, they threw themselves in crowds into those passes, and destroyed each other, from the fear of being destroyed by the *Romans*.

As *Cato* thought that a man had a right to boast of the great actions he had performed, he extols this last exploit in very pompous terms, and says, " That those who saw him
" rush

"rush on the enemy, rout and pursue them,
"acknowledged that *Cato* owed less to the
"people of *Rome*, than the people of *Rome*
"to *Cato*; and that *Manlius* the consul him-
"self returning hot from the fight, took him
"in his arms as he came panting and sweat-
"ing from the battle, and embracing him a
"long time, cried in a transport of joy, that
"neither he, nor all the people of *Rome*,
"could ever fully reward his services."

Cato being now sent by the consul to carry the news of his exploits to *Rome*, proceeded thither with the utmost expedition, and being the first that brought the news of this great victory, filled the city with joy and sacrifices; the people now imagining that they were able to subdue the whole earth.

These are the most extraordinary military actions performed by *Cato*. With respect to his conduct in civil affairs, he seems to have been persuaded, that the zeal of an honest man could not be better exerted, than in the prosecution of offenders; for he not only prosecuted several, but assisted others in carrying on prosecutions. He induced *Petilicus* to accuse the great *Scipio*, who being a person of high birth, and great magnanimity, treated their accusations with the utmost contempt: when *Cato* finding that he could not be capitally convicted, desisted from the prosecution, and joining with other accusers, attacked his brother *Lucius Scipio*, who being sentenced to pay a great fine, was in danger of being thrown into prison; but by appeal-

ing

ing to the tribunes, he was with great difficulty dismissed. Thus it is said, that a young man, having caused the enemy of his deceased father to be condemned, and crossing the market-place on the day when sentence was passed, *Cato* met him, and taking him by the hand, said, " These are the
" offerings we should make to the Manes of
" our deceased ancestors, to whom we should
" sacrifice, not the blood of goats and of
" lambs, but the condemnation and tears of
" their enemies."

He himself however did not escape; for in return, when ever his enemies could get the least hold of him, he was called to an account, so that there are said to have been near fifty accusations brought against him; the last of which happening when he was eighty six years of age, he complained, *That it was very hard he should be brought to justify to men of one generation, the actions he had performed in another.*

Ten years after he had enjoyed the office of consul, he stood for the post of Censor, which was the completion of all the dignities to which a *Roman* citizen could aspire. For the *Romans*, being convinced, that the dispositions of mankind are better discerned in the private affairs of life, than by actions of a public and political nature, chose two magistrates to be guardians, correctors, or reformers of manners, to prevent men's quitting the paths of virtue, for those of licentiousness and pleasure, and changing the

ancient

ancient and established customs. One of these was chosen out of the patricians, and the other from among the people. They might deprive a *Roman* knight of his horse, and expel from the senate any senator who lived a licentious and disorderly life. They likewise took an estimate of every citizen's estate, and kept an account of the several families, qualities, and conditions of people in the commonwealth.

As this office had several great prerogatives annexed to it, when *Cato* became a candidate for it, he was opposed by many considerable persons in the senate; some imagining, that it would be a disgrace to their nobility to suffer men of obscure birth to rise to the highest power and honour, and others, conscious of their own corrupt manners, opposed him, from their dread of his inexorable severity; they therefore set up seven candidates in opposition to him, who soothed the people with fair hopes and promises; while *Cato*, on the contrary, was far from using the least flattery; but threatening, from the chair in which he sat, all wicked men to their face, cried aloud, that the city wanted great reformation; conjured the people to chuse, not the mildest, but the severest physicians; and told them, that he himself was one of that character, and among the patricians *Valerius Flaccus* was another. On which the *Roman* people, so far from dreading his severity and rigour, rejected all the smooth flatterers who
appeared

appeared disposed to render their authority easy and popular, and unanimously chose *Cato* and *Valerius Flaccus.*

Cato began with naming *Lucius Valerius Flaccus* chief of the senate, and with removing several persons, particularly *Lucius Quintius*, who had been consul seven years before, and *Manlius* another senator, who stood fair for the consulship, was removed merely for giving his wife a kiss in open day, and in the presence of his daughter; *Cato* saying, that his wife never embraced him but in loud claps of thunder; and that he was happy when *Jupiter* thundered.

He was greatly censured for his usage of *Lucius*, the brother of the great *Scipio*; for, notwithstanding his being honoured with a triumph for his victory over king *Philip*, he took his horse from him, at a review of the *Roman* knights; merely, as it was thought, to insult the memory of *Scipio Africanus.* But nothing created so general a disgust, as his endeavouring to reform the prevailing luxury, by ordering all the apparel, vehicles, women's ornaments, furniture, and houshold goods to be appraised, and all that exceeded 1500 drachmas to be valued at ten times its worth. According to this valuation, he caused a tax of three asses to be paid for the value of every thousand asses, in order that they who found themselves heavily pressed, might be induced to lay aside their superfluities. Thus, he not only rendered those his enemies who chose to pay the tax

rather

rather than abandon their superfluities, but those who gave them up to avoid the tax. For people generally think, that being forbidden to shew their riches, is the same as taking them away; and that wealth is better seen in the superfluities, than the necessaries of life.

However, all the complaints and outcries made against *Cato*, had no other effect upon him, but to render him more rigid and severe. He demolished all such buildings as projected into the streets; ordered all the pipes by which private persons caused water to be conveyed from the public fountains to their houses and gardens, to be cut off; beat down the price of public works, and farmed out the public revenues at an excessive price: by which he procured the hatred of great numbers of people. Hence *Titus Flaminius*, and those of his party, caused the contracts he had made for repairing the temples and public buildings to be made void, and incited the tribunes to accuse him to the people, and fine him two talents. They also opposed his erecting a hall at the public expence, which he however finished, and gave it the name of the *Porcian Hall*. It however appears, that his conduct was highly approved by the people, since they raised a statue to him in the temple of *Health*, and the inscription on the base, instead of mentioning his battles, victories, and triumph, was as follows: " To the ho-
" nour of *Cato* the Censor, who, by good
" discipline, reclaimed the *Roman* common-
" wealth, when it was brought into danger,
" and

"and a declining state, by the public licentiousness."

He was both a good father and a good husband; for he was far from thinking, that his family deserved only a slight and superficial attention. He often said, that those who beat their wives or children laid violent hands on what was most sacred, and that he preferred the commendation of being an affectionate husband, before that of being a great senator. Whenever his wife was brought to bed, no business of a private nature could prevent his being present while she washed and swathed the child. His son was no sooner capable of instruction, than *Cato* himself became his instructor; for though *Chilo*, his slave, was not only an honest man, and a good grammarian, and had been employed in educating other children, he could not bear that his son should owe so great an obligation as his education to a slave. He himself was therefore his preceptor in grammar, law, and the gymnastic art; and taught him not only to ride, to throw the dart, and the use of the other military weapons; but even to box, to swim across a rapid river, and to endure heat and cold. He himself observes, that he wrote histories for him in large characters, with his own hand; that without quitting his father's house, he might be acquainted with the exploits and the laws of his ancestors; and he as carefully avoided all obscene discourse before him, as if he had been in the presence of the vestal virgins.

Thus

Thus *Cato* early trained up his son to virtue. He indeed found that he had an amiable disposition, and was fond of learning; but his body being too weak to undergo hard labour, his father was obliged to remit somewhat of the severity of his discipline. The weakness of his constitution did not, however, prevent his being a good soldier; for he particularly distinguished himself in the battle fought by *Paulus Æmilius* against *Perseus*, where his sword being struck out of his hand, he, by the assistance of his friends, cleared the place, and recovered it again *. This action was highly applauded by the general; and there is still extant a letter written by *Cato* to his son, wherein he commends his concern at losing his sword, and the bravery with which he recovered it.

While *Cato* was poor, he thought nothing more shameful than to quarrel with his slaves on the account of his belly; but, when his circumstances were mended, and he gave frequent entertainments to his friends, he, after the repast, always corrected with leathern thongs, those who had neglected to give due attendance, or had suffered any of the provisions to be spoiled. He also contrived means to set them at variance; for their having a good understanding among them, filled him with fear and suspicion; and, when any of them committed a crime worthy of death, he, on their being found

* See a more particular account of this event in the life of *Paulus Æmilius*, in vol. ii. p. 207.

guilty

guilty by their fellow-servants, punished them accordingly. His thirst for riches encreasing, he abandoned agriculture, for more lucrative employments, and purchased ponds, hot springs, pastures, and wood-lands; by which means he acquired a great revenue. He was guilty also of a very extraordinary kind of usury: he obliged those to whom he lent money on interest, to form themselves into a company, for instance, of fifty merchants, and to fit out fifty ships, wherein he had one share, which was taken care of by one of his freedmen, who sailed with them as his factor. He also lent money on usury to such of his slaves as had a mind to engage in trade; and, to incline his son to follow his example, he used to say, That he was worthy of immortal glory, who could shew by his accounts, that what he had added to his estate, exceeded what he had received from his ancestors.

Cato was far advanced in years, when two ambassadors arrived at *Rome* from *Athens*, *Carneades* the academic, and *Diogenes* the stoic. These philosophers were admired by the youth most distinguished for their learning, who heard them with inexpressible pleasure, and were particularly charmed with the graces and force of *Canneades*'s oratory: the greatest and most polite people in *Rome* were soon his auditors; and his fame, like a mighty wind, rushing thro' the city, it was every where said, that a *Greek* was arrived, who, by his eloquence, calmed the most turbulent passions, and inspired the *Roman* youth with such a love

of.

of wisdom, that renouncing business and diversions, they with an enthusiastic ardour applied themselves to the study of philosophy. Even the old men were highly pleased, and were filled with the utmost delight at seeing their youth thus eagerly receive the *Grecian* literature, and frequent the company of these extraordinary men. Their first discourses were translated into Latin by *Caius Acilius*, one of the chief of the senate, and universally spread abroad. *Cato*, however, was highly displeased, from his apprehensions lest the youth should prefer the glory of speaking to that of distinguishing themselves in arms; and therefore going to the senate, blamed the magistrates for detaining so long, ambassadors who could persuade the people to agree to whatever they pleased. "You "ought, said he, speedily to determine their "affair, that they may return to their schools, "and instruct the *Grecian* children, that the "*Roman* youth may be left to attend their "own laws and magistrates, as they did be"fore their arrival." This was not spoken out of any particular enmity to *Carneades*, but from *Cato's* being an enemy to philosophy, and his taking a pride in shewing that he despised the *Grecian* muses, and all foreign erudition; for he used to call even *Socrates* himself *a prating seditious fellow, who had endeavoured all in his power, to tyrannize over his country, by abrogating ancient customs, and leading his fellow citizens into new opinions, contrary to the laws*. And to dissuade his son from applying to any of the *Grecian* sciences,

he

he cried with a loud voice, as if filled with a prophetic spirit, *that the* Romans *would be destroyed when once they became infected with* Greek. Time has however sufficiently shewn the folly of this wayward prediction; for when the *Grecian* literature flourished at *Rome*, and all kind of learning was esteemed, that city was at the highest pitch of glory and power.

Nor was *Cato* less an enemy to the *Grecian* physicians than to their philosophers: for hearing that the king of *Persia* sent for *Hippocrates*, and offered him a reward of many talents; and that he answered, " I will never " make use of my skill in favour of Barba- " rians, who are enemies to the *Greeks*;" he asserted, that this was an oath taken by all physicians, and enjoined his son never to trust himself in their hands; adding, that he himself had written a small treatise, in which were several prescriptions, which he had used with good success when any of his family were sick, maintaining, that by the assistance of these remedies, with his regimen, he preserved himself, and all that belonged to him, in perfect health.

After the death of his wife, his son married the daughter of *Paulus Æmilius*; but he himself continued a widower, yet notwithstanding his being much advanced in years, he was far from observing the rules of continence; for he had an intrigue with a young slave. One day, as she was passing with a haughty air to *Cato*'s bed-chamber, his son, without speaking to her, gave her an angry look, and turned

turned from her with an air of indignation. This coming to the knowledge of the old man, he, on finding that his commerce with the slave was far from being agreeable either to his son, or his daughter-in-law, took no notice of what had passed; but the next morning early when he was going with his usual company to the Forum, he called aloud to one *Salonius*, who had been his secretary, asking him if his daughter was yet married. *Salonius* answered, That she was not, and never should, without his consent. Why then, I have found out a fit husband for her, replied *Cato*, provided she can bear with the inequality of age: he is in every other respect unexceptionable, but he is very old. The other then returned, that he left the disposal of her entirely to him; and *Cato*, without any farther ceremony cried, I will be thy son-in-law. *Salonius* was extremely suprized, and thinking himself much too mean, to have the least hopes of entering into an alliance with a person of consular dignity, no sooner found that *Cato* was in earnest, than he embraced the offer with great joy and thankfulness; and the marriage contract was signed as soon as they came to the Forum. While preparations were making for the nuptials, *Cato*'s son, attended by some of his friends and relations, went to his father, and asked him, What offence he had committed to induce him to give him a mother-in-law? On which *Cato* immediately replied, " There is " no offence, my son; in all thy behaviour " I find no cause of complaint. I am only
" desirous

"desirous of having more such sons, and of leaving my country more such citizens."

Cato had indeed a son by this second wife, whom he called *Salonius* from his mother's father. But his eldest son died in his prætorship. His father frequently mentions him in his works, as a person of extraordinary merit; yet he bore his loss with a philosophic temper, without suffering it to interrupt him in his application to affairs of state.

His causing the destruction of *Carthage* was the last affair of a public nature in which he engaged. *Massinissa*, king of *Numidia*, being at war with the *Carthaginians*, *Cato* was sent into *Africa* to learn the cause of their quarrel. *Massinissa* had been long the friend and ally of the *Romans*, and the *Carthaginians* had also been in alliance with them, ever since the great victory obtained by the elder *Scipio*, who stripped them of a considerable part of their dominions, and obliged them to pay a heavy tribute. *Cato*, on his arrival at *Carthage*, finding that city not in a low and declining condition, as the *Romans* imagined; but full of men capable of bearing arms, furnished with warlike stores, and abounding in wealth, returned hastily to *Rome*, where he told the senate, that all the misfortunes of the *Carthaginians* had rather cured them of their folly, than drained them of their forces; that the *Romans*, in their wars with them, instead of weakening, had rendered them more warlike and experienced; that their

battles

battles with the *Numidians* were only exercises by which they were trained up, that they might one day be able to cope with the *Romans*; that the late peace was a mere name, and nothing more than a suspension of arms; and that they only waited for a favourable opportunity to renew the war. At the conclusion of this speech, it is said, that he shook his gown, and purposely dropping some figs he had brought from *Africa*, they were taken up, and being admired for their beauty and largeness, he said, that the country where that fruit grew, was but three days sail from *Rome*. But his enmity to *Carthage* is more evidently shewn, in his never giving his opinion in the senate on any other subject, without concluding with the words, " It is my opinion that *Carthage* should be " destroyed [*]."

How-

---

[*] *Cato* the Censor is far from being an amiable character; but no action of his life, in the eye of reason and humanity, appears so inconsistent with every sentiment of justice and benevolence, as this conduct with respect to the *Carthaginians*. How poor was the artifice of dropping these figs, as a bait to the luxurious! How mean the fear, that made him dread a nation humbled by the calamities of war, lest in some future time they should again become formidable! And how unjust and cruel were his incessant endeavours, in the midst of peace, to

unsheath

However, no sooner was this third Punic war begun, which proved so fatal to Carthage, and which *Cato* had taken such pains to kindle, than he died, leaving behind him several histories, and other works on various subjects, particularly a book on country affairs; in which he treats of making cakes, and preserving fruit. He left one son by his second wife, who, as hath been already said, was called *Salonius*, and a grandson by the son of his first wife, who died before him. *Cato Salonius* dying during the time of his prætorship, left a son called *Marcus*, who was the father of *Cato* the philosopher, the greatest and best man of the age in which he lived.

Having related the most remarkable actions of *Aristides* and *Cato*, we find, upon carefully examining them, that they both advanced themselves by their virtue and abilities. It is true, *Aristides* appeared when *Athens* had not arisen to its utmost splendor, and when its chief magistrates were possessed of only moderate fortunes. But *Cato*, from a petty village, and a country life, launched into the commonwealth, at a time when the greatness of family, distributions among the people, and courting their favour with the utmost servility, were alone regarded; for the

unsheath the sword, in order to extirpate a people only because it might be done with safety!

Romans, being elated with the strength and stability of the commonwealth, took delight in humbling those who were candidates for any preferment.

With respect to their military glory, *Aristides* was never commander in chief in any action; for *Miltiades* obtained the victory at *Marathon*; *Themistocles* at *Salamis*; and *Pausanias* at *Plataeae*. While *Cato* obtained the chief praise for his conduct and courage, not only in the *Spanish* war, in which he commanded, as consul; but at *Thermopylae*, when he had only the post of tribune, he acquired the glory of the victory, by opening a way for the *Romans* to rush in upon *Antiochus*, and attack his troops in the rear: for that victory was indisputably *Cato*'s work. Yet *Cato* added but little to the *Roman* empire, which was then very extensive; but the warlike expeditions, in which *Aristides* was engaged, are the noblest and most important actions the *Greeks* ever performed. The demolition of the walls of the *Spanish* towns, and the defeat of *Antiochus*, cannot be compared with the destruction of so many thousand *Persians* both by sea and land in the war with *Xerxes*. In all these noble exploits, *Aristides* was inferior to none in valour; but he left the glory and the laurels, as well as the wealth and money, to those who desired them more: for he was above them. *Cato* was perpetually boasting, and preferring himself to all others, though in one of his orations he acknowledges, that it is equally absurd either to

praise

praise or dispraise one's self. Modesty indeed greatly contributes to that mildness of temper which so well becomes a statesman, but the pride and ambition of *Cato* rendered his temper harsh and morose. *Aristides* by generously assisting *Themistocles*, his enemy, and acting as an officer under him, had the glory of contributing to restore the city of *Athens*; while *Cato*, by opposing *Scipio*, almost defeated his expedition against the *Carthaginians*, and at last, by continually calumniating him, made him retire from *Rome*. With respect to the most amiable virtues, justice, temperance, and humanity, *Aristides* had the advantage; but he carried his disinterestedness too far; for justice does not require that a man should be useful to others, and pay no regard to the interest of himself and his family. The temperance and frugality of both were commendable; but to what purpose did *Cato* hoard up wealth which he did not dare to use? or what motive but the extremest avarice could he have to employ so many arts of acquiring wealth, while he esteemed boiled turnips most delicious food.

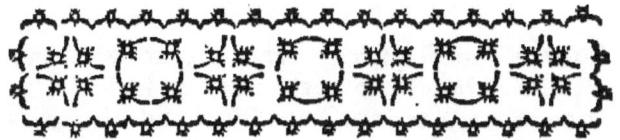

THE
LIFE
OF
PHILOPOEMEN.

CRAUSIS, the father of *Philopœmen*, had a sincere friendship for *Cassander*, whom he entertained with great splendor in his house at *Megalopolis*; in return, *Cassander*, after the death of *Crausis*, endeavoured to repay the father's hospitable kindness, by the care he took in the education of *Philipœmen*, his orphan son, whom he caused to be trained up to the precepts of philosophy.

Philipœmen had an insatiable ambition, and was somewhat rough and choleric. He strove to resemble *Epaminondas*, and was not much inferior to him in valour, conduct, and incorruptible integrity: he had even from
his

his childhood a strong propensity to war, and applied himself to such arts as had a relation to it, as horsemanship, and the management of his weapons. When he began to bear arms in the incursions which his fellow-citizens used to make against the *Spartans* for the sake of pillage, he would always march out the first, and return the last. At his leisure time he endeavoured to add to his strength and activity by hunting, and labouring in his grounds, he having a good estate about twenty furlongs from the town. At break of day he usually went to work, either in his vineyard, or at the plough, from which he returned to the town, and employed his time in public business, with his friends, or the magistrates; he returned to his farm every day after dinner and supper, and at night threw himself on the first mattrass, where he slept till morning. He also spent much of his time in hearing the discourses, and studying the writings of philosophers, and of such authors as treated on the art of war, and the manner of drawing up an army in order of battle. He was indeed too much addicted to war, and had a contempt for all who were not soldiers; but he endeavoured to improve his estate, that he might be free from all temptation of wronging others.

When he was thirty years of age, *Cleomenes*, king of *Sparta*, surprised *Megolopolis* by night. *Philopœmen* ran to assist his fellow-citizens; but tho' he was unable to drive the enemy out

out of the town, he made head againſt them, and gave the citizens time to eſcape. His horſe was killed under him; and having received ſeveral wounds, he himſelf eſcaped with difficulty, and was the laſt man in the retreat. They all retired to *Meſſene*, where *Cleomenes* ſent to let them know, that he would reſtore their town, their goods, and their territory. They were pleaſed with the offer, and eager to return; but *Philopœmen* prevented them by repreſenting, that what he called reſtoring the city, was taking the citizens, in order to keep the place with the greater ſecurity; but that he would not ſtay long to guard empty houſes. *Cleomenes*, however, deſtroyed great part of the city, and carried away much booty.

King *Antigonus* coming ſome time after to ſuccour the *Achæans*, they united their forces, and marched againſt *Cleomenes*, who had ſeized the avenues, and was advantageouſly poſted on the hills of *Sellaſia*. *Antigonus* drew up his army, in order to force him from his poſt. *Philopœmen*, with his citizens, was placed among the horſe, ſupported by the *Illyrian* foot, who cloſed one of the wings. They were ordered to keep their ground, and not to engage, till they ſaw a red robe lifted up on the point of a ſpear, in the other wing, where the king fought in perſon. Theſe orders were obeyed by the *Achæans*; but the *Illyrian* infantry fell briſkly upon the enemy, and *Euclidas*, the brother of *Cleomenes*, obſerving the foot thus ſeparated from the horſe, ordered a body of light armed troops to wheel about,

about, and charge the *Illyrians* behind. This threw them into confusion: when *Philopœmen*, considering that the light armed troops might be easily dispersed, went to the king's officers to propose the performance of it; but looking on him as a rash inconsiderate young man, they paid no regard to his advice. He therefore attacked those troops with his own citizens, and soon put them to flight, with a great slaughter. Then to encourage the army to make a general attack, while the enemy were in confusion, he dismounted; but while he was thus fighting, in his heavy horseman's armour, on rough uneven ground, full of springs, both his thighs were struck through with a javelin, so that the point came out on the other side. He stood as if he had been shackled, and was unable to move; for the thong in the middle of the weapon rendered it difficult to be drawn out. But the battle being now at the hottest, his impatience to be engaged, enabled him to make such efforts to move his legs, that he at last broke the staff, and ordering the pieces to be pulled out, ran with his sword through the midst of those who were fighting in the first ranks, animating the men, and firing them with emulation.

This action brought *Philopœmen* into great reputation, and *Antigonus* offered him very advantageous conditions to engage him to enter into his service. But *Philopœmen* hearing there was a war in *Crete*, went thither, and having spent a considerable time in that island,

island, with men distinguished for their bravery, and military knowledge, returned with such fame, that the *Achæans* immediately chose him general of the horse. Their cavalry had at that time neither experience nor courage; they rode on little horses, the cheapest they could procure, and when the men were to march, they commonly hired others to serve in their stead, while they staid at home. *Philopœmen* endeavoured to inspire all the young men with martial ardour: he continually reviewed and exercised them, and by making them frequently engage in mock skirmishes, rendered them strong and bold, active and vigorous. By use they acquired such command of their horses, and obtained such readiness in their various evolutions, whether performed separately or together, that the whole number resembled a single body actuated by an internal principle. In a great battle which the *Achæans* fought with the *Eleans* and *Ætolians*, near the river *Larissus*, *Damophantus*, general of the *Elean* horse, singled out *Philopœmen*, and rode up to him full speed; but *Philopœmen* prevented the blow, by striking him dead with his spear; and from thence forward was universally celebrated as one who in personal valour yielded not to the youngest, nor to the oldest in good conduct, and all the qualities of a general.

The *Achæans* formerly used light, thin, and narrow bucklers, and short javelins; but he introduced a larger buckler, and the
long

long pike, and perſuaded them to arm their heads, bodies, thighs, and legs; and inſtead of looſe ſkirmiſhing, to fight firmly foot to foot. Having thus brought them all to wear armour, he turned their fondneſs for dreſs and idle expence, to the deſire of making a fine appearance in their warlike equipage. Nothing then was to be ſeen in the ſhops but artificers employed in making breaſt-plates, bucklers, and bridles adorned with gold and ſilver; nothing in the places of exerciſes, but young men riding and exerciſing their arms; while the women were frequently ſeen embroidering military veſts for both the cavalry and infantry. Mean while the ſight of their rich armour raiſed their ſpirits, and quickened their courage: they wore it with pleaſure, and by conſtant uſe it became light and eaſy, and they longed for nothing more than to try it with an enemy.

At that time the *Achæans* were at war with *Machanidas*, tyrant of *Sparta*, who watched all opportunities of rendering himſelf maſter of all *Peloponneſus*. On his attacking the *Mantineans*, *Philopœmen* marched againſt him. They met near *Mantinea*, and drew up in ſight of that city, having not only the whole ſtrength of their ſeveral cities, but a conſiderable number of mercenaries. At the beginning of the battle, *Machanidas*, with his hired troops, broke thro' the ſpearmen and *Tarentines* placed by *Philopœmen* in the front to cover the *Achæans*; and having
put

put them to flight, followed the chace without attacking the *Achæan* army, which stood firm. At this unfortunate beginning, the rest of the confederates gave themselves over for lost; but *Philopæmen* seemed to slight it as of small consequence, and suffered *Machanidas* to pursue the fugitives till he was at a great distance, and then suddenly charged the *Lacedæmonians*, who were deserted by their horse, and without a commander. Thus *Philopæmen* overthrew them with a great slaughter, above 4000 being said to be killed on the spot. He then faced about against *Machanidas*, who was returning with his mercenaries from the pursuit. There happened to be a broad ditch between them, into which *Machanidas*'s horse, feeling the spur, ventured to leap: but as he was mounting the other side, *Philopæmen* rode up, and striking *Machanidas* with all his force, tumbled him dead into the ditch. The *Achæans* were so pleased with this victory, and the success of this single combat, that they erected a brazen statue to *Philopæmen* at *Delphi*, in the posture in which he killed the tyrant.

A little after this victory, *Philopæmen* being at the *Nemean* games, shewed his army drawn up in order of battle with all their exercises and evolutions, after which he entered the theatre, while the musicians were singing for the prize, attended by a number of his soldiers dressed in their military vests, and scarlet tunics. At their coming in, one

Pylades

PHILOPÆMEN kills MACHANIDAS Tyrant of Sparta.

Pylades was accidentally singing this verse out of the *Persæ* of *Timotheus.*

Glory and freedom Greece *from me receives.*

The whole theatre cast their eyes on *Philopœmen,* and clapped their hands, being transported with the hopes of recovering their former glory.

Philip, king of *Macedon,* imagining that *Philopœmen* would be the only obstacle to his bringing the *Achæans* into subjection, privately sent some persons to *Argos* to assassinate him; but this base design being discovered, it only served to render him infamous, and the object of the hatred of all *Greece.* When the *Bœotians* were besieging *Megara,* and were ready to storm the town, on a groundless rumour, that *Philopœmen* was coming with succours, they fled, leaving their scaling-ladders fastened to the walls. *Nabis,* who, after the death of *Machanidas,* became tyrant of *Sparta* had surprised *Messene* at a time when *Philopœmen* was out of command, and that great man endeavoured to persuade *Lysippus,* the *Achæan* general, to succour *Messene;* but the place being taken, he considered it as entirely lost. On this *Philopœmen* resolved to go without any commission, only followed by his own citizens, who considered him as formed for command: and *Nabis* no sooner heard of his approach, than he stole off with his army at the farther gate of

the

the city, thinking himself happy in being able to make his escape, and *Philopœmen* entered it without opposition.

He afterwards entered into the service of the *Gortynians* in the isle of *Crete*, where he made war not openly in the field; but fought the *Cretans* at their own weapons, turning their stratagems against themselves, and soon made them sensible that they were only like children using low and trifling arts against a man of wisdom and experience. Having managed the war with great bravery and reputation, he returned to *Peloponnesus*, where *Philip* had been defeated by *Titus Quintius*, and *Nabis* was at war both with the *Romans* and *Achæans*. He was soon chosen general against *Nabis*; but venturing a battle by sea, had the disadvantage, and the enemy elated with their victory, laid siege to *Gythium*. *Philopœmen* no sooner heard of this, than he sailed towards that town, and landing in the night, when they had no suspicion of his approach, killed many of the enemy, and burnt their camp.

As he was marching a few days after thro' some narrow passes, *Nabis* suddenly came upon him. The *Achæans* were struck with fear and consternation, and despaired of ever escaping: but *Philopœmen* making a halt, viewed the ground, and then advancing only a few paces, and changing the position of his troops, according to the nature of the place, removed all apprehensions from his men, and then charging, put the enemy to
flight

flight. When seeing that they did not fly towards the city, but dispersed themselves about the country, which was very woody and uneven, he sounded a retreat, and encamped by broad day-light; then foreseeing that the enemy would endeavour in the dark to steal separately into the city, he posted strong parties of the *Achæans* near the walls, and by this means many of them fell into their hands; for *Nabis*'s men returning as the chance of flight had dispersed them, were caught like birds ere they could enter the place.

The bravery and conduct of *Philopœmen* were now celebrated in all the theatres of *Greece*. *Nabis* being at length slain by the *Ætolians*, every thing at *Sparta* was thrown into confusion, and *Philopœmen* seizing this opportunity, advanced thither with his army, and by the united force of persuasion and fear, brought the whole city under the subjection of the *Achæans*. His behaviour on this occasion was such, that he gained the esteem of the *Spartans* themselves, who hoped that he would be the friend and defender of their liberty: and having raised 120 talents by the sale of *Nabis*'s house and effects, they decreed that the money should be presented to him; but so high an opinion had the people of *Philopœmen*'s virtue and disinterestedness, that none among them cared to mention it to him. At length this commission was intrusted to *Timolaus*, with whom *Philopœmen* had lodged at *Sparta;* and in return he went to *Megalopolis*, where he was entertained by *Philopœmen*; but being ſtruck with admiration at his frugality and integrity, he judged that he was not to be tempted by money, and therefore pretending other buſineſs, returned without mentioning a word of the preſent. Being ſent again, he acted juſt as before; but the third time he with much difficulty informed *Philopœmen* of the teſtimony the city of *Sparta* had given him of their regard. That great man hearkened to him with pleaſure, and then going with him to *Sparta*, adviſed the people not to bribe their friends, on whoſe virtue they might depend without expence: but to buy off thoſe bad men who were perpetually diſturbing the city with their ſeditious ſpeeches.

The *Achæans* having afterwards made *Diophanes* their general, he reſolved to chaſtiſe the *Spartans*, whom he heard were raiſing new commotions: upon which they, preparing for war, embroiled all *Pelopenneſus*. *Philopœmen* endeavoured to make *Diephanes* ſenſible, that while *Antiochus* and the *Romans* were contending with powerful armies in the heart of *Greece*, he ought to diſſemble and paſs by many injuries to keep all quiet at home. But *Diephanes* joining with *Titus Flaminius*, the *Roman* general, marched directly to *Sparta*, on which *Philopœmen* getting into the town, though a private man, kept out both the *Roman* conſul and the general of *Achæa*, and having appeaſed the diſturbances in the city, again united it to the *Achæans*.

But

But afterwards the *Lacedæmonians* rebelling again while *Philopæmen* himself was general, he put to death, according to *Polybius*, eighty, or according to *Aristocrates*, 350 citizens, razed the walls, and gave a confiderable part of their territory to the *Megalopolitans*. He likewife carried to *Achæa* all who had been made free of *Sparta* by the tyrants, except 3000, who would not fubmit to banifhment, and thofe he cruelly fold for flaves; and abrogating the laws of *Lycurgus*, forced them to educate their youth after the manner of the *Achæans*. But this reftraint was of fhort duration; for by the confent of the *Romans*, they foon forfook the *Achæan* cuftoms, and as much as poffible re-eftablifhed their ancient difcipline.

When *Antiochus* was overcome, the *Romans* preffed harder upon *Greece*, and furrounding the *Achæans* with their forces, the leading men in the feveral cities went over to their intereft. Upon this occafion *Philopæmen* fometimes yielded to the neceffity of the times; but generally continued fteady, and ufed his utmoft endeavours to keep all who were confiderable either for their wealth or eloquence, firm in the defence of their common liberty. After the defeat of *Antiochus*, Manius the Roman conful, endeavoured to perfuade the *Achæans* to fuffer the banifhed *Spartans* to return to their country; but this was oppofed by *Philopæmen*, who was not willing that they fhould be obliged to the *Romans*: but the next

next year, when he himself was general, he permitted them to go to *Sparta*.

Philopœmen being now seventy years old, and the eighth time general, was in hopes of passing the rest of his days in quiet: but these hopes were vain. It is said, that hearing a great commander praised, he replied, that there was no great account to be made of a man, who had suffered himself to be taken alive by his enemies. But how blind is man with respect to futurity! A few days after, hearing that *Dinocrates*, a *Messenian*, and his particular enemy, had induced the *Messenians* to revolt from the *Achæans*, and was about to seize a small town called *Colonis*, notwithstanding his being ill, he hasted to *Megalopolis*, and took from thence a choice body of horse, composed of the chief persons in the city, who from their affection to him, and their love of glory, desired to accompany him. They marched towards *Messene*, and meeting with *Dinocrates*, charged and routed him; but a body of 500 fresh men coming to his relief, the enemy rallied; and *Philopœmen* fearing that he should be surrounded, retreated, bringing up the rear in person, none of the enemy daring to approach near him. Being desirous of saving every man, he so often faced about, that he was at last left alone amidst a great number of his enemies, who attacking him at a distance with their darts, drove him up to steep and stony places, where his horse could scarcely pass. He was weakened with sickness and fatigue, and his horse

horse at last stumbling, threw him, when receiving a wound in his head, he lay speechless; and the enemy thinking him dead, began to strip him: but soon seeing him lift up his head, and open his eyes, they rushed in crowds upon him, bound his hands behind him, and led him away, insulting him with the most opprobrious language.

The *Messenians*, on his approach, thronged to the gates of the city: but no sooner saw *Philopœmen* appear in a manner so unsuitable to the glory of his great exploits, than struck with the vanity and inconstancy of *Fortune*, many of them wept, and began to offer him consolation, adding, that they ought to remember that they owed their liberty to him when he drove away *Nabis*. While a few, to pay their court to *Dinocrates*, were for tormenting and putting him to death. These thrust him into a dark dungeon under ground, which having no doors, was covered with a stone; this was instantly rolled to the mouth of the dungeon, and having placed a guard about it they left him.

Mean while *Philopœmen*'s men recovering themselves after their flight, and fearing he was dead, since they could not see him; made a stand, calling him with loud cries, and reproaching each other for suffering their general to lose his life, in endeavouring to preserve theirs. After making a diligent search, and a strict enquiry, they at last heard that he was taken, when they soon spread the news through all the towns in *Achæa*. The

Achæans deeply afflicted at this misfortune, sent to demand him, and at the same time assembled their army, for his rescue.

Dinocrates, however, fearing that *Philopœmen* would be saved, resolved to be beforehand with the *Achæans*; and therefore, as soon as night had dispersed the multitude, he sent in the executioner with poison, ordering him not to leave him till he had taken it. He found *Philopœmen* lying down wrapt in his cloak, and oppressed with grief and trouble. On his seeing the light, and the man standing by him with the poison, he sat up, and taking the cup, asked him if he had heard any thing of his body of horse, and particularly of *Lycortas*? he answered, that most of them had got off safe. At this *Philopœmen* smiling, cried, " It is well that we are not every way " unfortunate;" and drinking up the poison, laid himself down again, and soon expired.

All *Achæa* were afflicted at the news of his death, and the youth, with some of the principal persons of the several cities met at *Megalopolis*, with the resolution to take immediate revenge. *Lycortas* was chosen general, who attacking the *Messenians* ravaged their country, till by common consent they submitted to the *Achæans*. *Dinocrates* killed himself to prevent his falling into their hands. Those who voted for *Philopœmen*'s death, were slain by the *Achæans*, and those who proposed his being tormented, were carried away as prisoners. Having burnt his body, and put his ashes into an urn, they
marched

marched home with a mixture of triumphal and funeral pomp, wearing crowns of victory on their heads, and attended by their captives in fetters. The urn was carried by *Polybius*, the general's son, but it was so covered with garlands and ribbons, that scarce any of it could be seen. The people from all the towns and villages in the way, flocked to meet them, and saluting and touching the urn, joined the procession, and went to *Megalopolis*, where the old men, with the women and children, mingled with the rest; and the whole city was filled with cries and lamentations for the loss of *Philopæmen*. Thus he was honourably interred: the prisoners were there stoned by his monument: after which many statues were erected, and other honours decreed him by the several cities.

THE LIFE OF T. Q. FLAMINIUS.

TITUS *Quintus Flaminius*, whom we chuse for a parallel to *Philopœmen*, was warm in his enmity and his friendship, but his anger was soon appeased; and he was constant and indefatigable in conferring benefits. Those whom he had obliged, he treated with as much civility and respect, as if the obligation had been conferred on himself. He was desirous of performing the best and the greatest actions, and received more pleasure from those who needed his assistance, than from those who were capable of serving him; considering the former as objects on which he might exert his virtue, and the latter as his competitors in glory.

As

As *Rome* was then engaged in many wars, her youth applied themselves to arms, and *Titus* was early taught the art of war. He was tribune under the consul *Marcellus*, who was cut off in an ambuscade laid by *Hannibal*; and afterwards obtaining the government of *Tarentum*, and the adjacent country, became as distinguished for his administration of justice as for his military skill, which occasioned his being chosen leader of the two colonies sent to the cities of *Cossa* and *Naruia*. This inspired him with loftier thoughts, and he endeavoured to pass over the previous offices of tribune of the people, prætor and ædile, to aspire immediately to the consulship: *Fulvius* and *Manlius*, tribunes of the people, alledged the indecency of suffering so young a man, who was not yet initiated into the first mysteries of government, to intrude, in contempt of the laws, into the sovereign power: but the senate remitting the affair to the choice of the people, they elected him consul with *Sextus Ælius*, though he was not thirty years of age.

The war against *Philip* king of *Macedon* fell by lot to *Titus*, which was extremely fortunate to the *Romans*, as the drawing the other states from the assistance of that prince, required a general who could employ the methods of mildness and persuasion, rather than one who would endeavour to succeed merely by violence and war. *Greece* had hitherto held but little correspondence with the *Romans*, and only then begun to concern itself

self with their affairs; and therefore would have been more averse to embracing a foreign authority, had not *Titus* been endued with an humane disposition, an insinuating address, and above all, a constant regard to justice.

Titus perceived that *Sulpitius* and *Publius*, his predecessors in that command, had trifled away a great part of the year in ostentation of their new acquired honours, and in the administration of civil affairs; after which, in the close of the year, they joined the army, and by this artifice prolonged their dignity another year, acting the consul in the first, and the general in the latter. But *Titus* slighting these domestic honours, and solely bent on the vigorous prosecution of the war, requested the senate that the command of the fleet might be given to his brother *Lucius*, and took with him a body of chosen troops, consisting of three thousand of those who under *Scipio* had defeated *Asdrubal* in *Spain*, and *Hannibal* in *Africa*. With these forces he got safe to *Epirus* [*], where he found *Publius* encamped opposite to *Philip*, who had long possessed the passage over the river *Apsus*, and the streights there, while *Publius*, from the natural strength of the place, was unable to effect any thing against him. *Titus* therefore taking upon himself the command of the army, dismissed *Publius*,

[*] Now a province of *Turky* in *Europe* called *Canina*, situated near the entrance of the gulph of *Venice*.

and

and began with enquiring into the nature of the country.

Epirus is no less mountainous than *Tempe*; but the country is inferior to it in beauty, it not being so finely diversified with the delightful verdure of trees, groves, meadows, and fields. The bed of the river *Apsus* extends between great and lofty mountains, which rising on each side like vast banks, form a deep and large channel, which in its appearance, and the swiftness of its current nearly resembles the river *Peneus*. It extends on each side to the foot of the hills, leaving only a craggy narrow path cut close by the stream, difficult at any time to be passed by an army; but absolutely impassable when guarded by an enemy.

Titus was advised to take a compass along the river *Lycus*, which was an easy passage: but being afraid, that if he should remove into barren and almost uncultivated countries, and *Philip* should then decline fighting, he might be forced, through want of provisions, to return to the sea shore, without performing any thing, as his predecessor had done before him, he resolved to force his way over the mountains: but *Philip* having possessed them, from all parts showered down darts and arrows on the *Romans*, and there happened several skirmishes, in which many were kill'd and wounded on both sides: but yet this afforded no prospect of ending the war. At length, some men, who fed their cattle on those eminences, came to inform *Titus*, that there was a way, which,

which, by taking a circuit, led to the top of the hills, and which the enemy had neglected to guard; and by this way they offered to conduct the army within three days at farthest to the top of the mountains. To gain the surer credit, they alledged, that *Charops*, king of *Epirus*, was not only privy to their design, but would make good all they had promised. This prince was a friend to the *Romans*, and gave them assistance, though he did it privately for fear of *Philip*.

Titus placing confidence in him, sent a captain with 300 horse and 4000 foot: but the herdsmen, who were their guides, were kept in bonds. They marched in the night by the light of the moon, which was then at full; and in the day-time lay still under the covert of hollow and woody places. *Titus* now remained inactive, and had only some slight skirmishes with the enemy to keep them employed. But on the day when the party he had detached were expected on the top of the mountain, he early drew up his troops, and forming them into three divisions, led the van, marching along the narrow pass by the side of the river. The *Macedonians* assaulted him at a distance with their darts; mean while the two other squadrons, with prodigious courage and alacrity, clinging to the rocks, endeavoured to come to action. When the sun was up, a thin smoke appeared afar off, like the mists that usually hang on the mountains, which was unperceived by the enemy, because it was behind them; for it
was

was caused by the troops who had already gained the summit of the eminences. The *Romans* were however yet in suspence; but as it increased in thickness, obscured the air, and rose to a greater height, they no longer doubted its being made by their companions; when giving a loud shout, and clambering up resolutely, they drove the enemy to the most craggy places. Those behind the enemy now echoed back the shouts of their friends from the top of the mountain, and the *Macedonians* immediately fled; but the difficulties of the place not allowing a long and close pursuit, there were not more than 2000 of them slain. The *Romans* however, pillaged their camp, seized on their wealth and slaves, and became absolute masters of the passes; after which they traversed all *Epirus*, without offering the least injury to the inhabitants.

Titus being afterwards informed, that *Philip*, who rather fled than marched through *Thessaly* *, forced the inhabitants to take shelter in the mountains, that he burnt the towns, and gave the goods, which the people could not carry off, to be plundered by his troops, earnestly intreated the army to pass through that coun-

---

* That country now called *Janna*, is at present a province of *Turky* in *Europe*; bounded by *Macedonia* on the north; by *Epirus* on the west; by *Achaia* or *Livadia* on the south, and by the *Archipelago* on the east.

try, as if it were their own; and indeed they soon perceived the benefit they derived from following the humane advice of their general: for they no sooner entered *Theſſaly*, than the cities surrendered to them; the *Grecians* within *Thermopylæ* ardently longed to put themselves under the protection of *Titus*; and the *Achæans*, breaking their league with *Philip*, joined the *Romans* against him. For those who had heard *Titus* represented by the *Macedonians*, as an invader at the head of an army of Barbarians, carrying every where slavery and destruction, were struck with surprize and pleasure, at seeing on the contrary, a man of a mild and graceful aspect, in the flower of his age, who in his voice and language was a *Grecian*, and who in all his actions shewed that he was a man of honour and humanity: they could not help being charmed with him, and on leaving him, filled the cities to which they came with affection and esteem for his person. Afterwards, when *Philip* seemed inclined to an accommodation, *Titus* offered him peace and the friendship of the *Romans*, on condition of his withdrawing his garrisons, and leaving the *Grecians* their own laws and liberties; but this he refused, and it was evident to all, and even to *Philip*'s party, that the *Romans* came not to fight against the *Greeks*, but only to defend them from the *Macedonians*.

All the rest of *Greece* having voluntarily submitted to him, except *Bœotia*, he marched into that country without committing any
act

act of hostility. The nobility and chief men of *Thebes* * came to meet him; and, though they favoured the *Macedonians*, they paid their compliments to *Titus*, for they were in friendship with both parties. They were received by *Titus* in the most courteous and obliging manner, who entering into discourse with them, proceeded slowly on, to allow time for those of his soldiers, who were behind, to come up with him. In this manner he entered the city with the *Thebans*; for tho' it was against their inclinations, they durst not deny him entrance; and *Titus* still continued his discourse, and persuaded them to join the *Romans*, as if the city had not been at his mercy. Thus he induced the *Bœotians* to side with the *Romans*.

Philip afterwards sending an embassy to *Rome*, *Titus* also sent agents on his part, to sollicit the senate to allow him still to have the command, if the war continued; and if they determined to put a period to it, to grant him the honour of concluding the peace. On which his friends took such measures, that *Philip* could obtain none of his demands, and *Titus* was allowed to continue the war.

* This ancient city was seated near the place where *Thiva* now stands, in *Turky* in *Europe*, and ought not to be confounded with the celebrated *Thebes* in *Upper Egypt*; of which a very curious account is given in *The World displayed*, vol. xii. p. 145, &c.

Titus was no sooner informed of the senate's determination, than he marched back into *Thessaly* to make head against *Philip*. His army consisted of 26,000 men, of which the *Ætolians* furnished 6000 foot and 400 horse, and the forces of *Philip* amounted to about the same number. Both armies advanced to meet each other till they came near *Scotusa*, where they resolved to hazard a battle. On this occasion *Titus* exhorted his soldiers to exert all their bravery, as they were now to contend in the midst of *Greece*, the most glorious theatre in the world, with adversaries distinguished for their strength and valour. On the other hand, *Philip* mounted an eminence on the outside of his camp, in order to his being the better heard, and began to harangue his men; but they were instantly seized with the most dreadful despondency; because the place on which he stood was a burying-ground, which they considered as a fatal omen. This circumstance gave *Philip* such concern, that he returned to his camp, and declined fighting all day.

The night was rainy, and the next morning, when there was a thick fog, both *Titus* and *Philip* sending out parties to make discoveries, and form ambuscades, they fell in with each other, and engaged at a narrow pass called *Cynocephalæ*, or the *Dogs Heads*, which are sharp peaks on the tops of the hills, standing thick and close to each, and gained the name from their shape having some resemblance to that of a dog's head. These skirmishes

mishes were attended with various success, as might be expected in such uneven places; the same party being sometimes hot in the pursuit, and sometimes flying, each general sent succours from his camp, as he saw his own men pressed and giving way: till at length, the sky clearing up, the whole armies engaged. *Philip*, who commanded the right wing, advanced from the rising ground with his whole phalanx against the *Romans*, the bravest of whom were unable to withstand the force of their united shields and projected spears, their left wing was therefore broken; which being observed by *Titus*, who had little hopes on that side, he hasted to the other, and there charged the *Macedonians*, who, from the inequality and roughness of the country, could neither keep their body entire, nor line their ranks, but were obliged to fight man to man, under heavy and unweildy armour. For the *Macedonian* phalanx, while it continues united in one body, and shield is locked to shield, resembles an animal of enormous strength; but being once broken, every single soldier of which it is composed, loses a part of his own strength from the nature of his armour; for each is strong, only as he forms a part of the whole. These being therefore soon routed, some gave chace to those who fled, while others charged those *Macedonians* in flank who were still fighting; and thus the victorious wing was soon broken and put to flight. No less than 8000 were slain, and about 5000 taken

taken prisoners; and had it not been for the *Ætolians*, *Philip* himself would probably not have escaped: for instead of joining the *Romans* in the pursuit, they fell to plundering the camp, and carried off all the booty before they returned. This occasioned great quarrels: but afterwards they offended *Titus* still more, by ascribing the victory to themselves, and prepossessing the *Grecians* by reports to their own advantage; so that, in the songs that were made on this action, the *Ætolians* were ranked first. *Titus* was very ambitious of acquiring a reputation among the *Greeks*; he however only shewed his resentment by managing every thing without the *Ætolians*; at which they were so offended, that when *Titus* listened to terms of accommodation, and admitted of an embassy from the king of *Macedon*, they exclaimed in all the *Grecian* cities, that this peace was purchased by *Philip*, though it was in *Titus*'s power to put a final period to the war, and to lay waste that empire which had enslaved all *Greece*. But while the *Ætolians* laboured to shake the fidelity of the *Roman* confederates, by these and the like reports, *Philip*, by suing for peace, and submitting himself and his kingdom to the *Romans*, removed all these jealousies.

Thus *Titus* put a period to the war; but, though he re-instated *Philip* in the kingdom of *Macedon*, he obliged him to quit *Greece*, and fined him 1000 talents; he also deprived him of all his vessels, and sent *Demetrius*, one of of his sons, hostage to *Rome*. For *Hannibal*, who had fled from his own country, had long taken up his residence at the court of king *Antiochus*, a victorious prince, whom he excited to take up arms against the *Romans*; and had he joined his troops to those of *Philip*, these two princes, who were the greatest and most powerful of that age, *Rome* might once more have been exposed to the same hazard, and have been reduced to the same extremities, as those she had suffered in the wars against *Hannibal*; but, by the timely conclusion of this peace, he at once disappointed *Antiochus* of his first hopes, and *Philip* of his last refuge.

In the mean time, there arrived ten commissioners, sent by the senate to *Titus*, with orders to advise him to restore the rest of *Greece* to liberty; but to keep garrisons in *Corinth*, *Chalcis* and *Demetrias*, as a security against any attempt from *Antiochus*. Hence the *Ætolians*, who were always famed for calumny, took occasion to raise commotions, calling on *Titus* to knock off the *Shackles* of *Greece*; (for so *Philip* used to term those three cities) and they asked the *Grecians*, Whether it was not a great consolation to them, that, while their chains weighed heavier, they were neater and better polished than formerly? And whether *Titus* did not deserve to be admired as their benefactor, who had unshackled the feet of *Greece*, and tied her up by the neck?

Titus,

Titus, though highly provoked, prevailed on the council to have those garrisons removed. Just at this time were celebrated the *Isthmian* games, and the theatre was crowded with multitudes who sat to see the exercises, when the crier stepping forth amidst the spectators, made proclamation, "That the *Ro-*
"*man* senate, and *Titus Quintius* the pro-
"consular general, having vanquished king
"*Philip* and the *Macedonians*, restored the
"*Corinthians*, *Locrians*, *Phocians*, *Eubæans*,
"*Achæans*, *Pthiotæ*, *Magnesians*, *Thessalians*,
"and *Perræbians*, to their liberty, took off
"all impositions, and withdrew their gar-
"risons." Instantly there arose a strange murmur and commotion in the theatre; some shewing signs of joy and astonishment; some asking questions, and others calling out to the crier to repeat it again. A profound silence was now made, and every ear fixed in attention. The crier then raised his voice; he was heard by the whole assembly; and the proclamation was no sooner ended, than in an extasy of joy, they gave a shout so incredibly loud, that it was heard as far as the sea. All the people rose up, unanimously embraced each other, and saluted *Flaminius* as the saviour and deliverer of *Greece*. The wonderful effects ascribed to the strength of the united voices of a vast multitude were here verified; for some crows that happened to be flying over the stage, fell down dead upon the shout.

FLAMINIUS restoring Liberty to Greece.

Vast multitudes crowded about *Titus* to express their joy and their acknowledgments; but he withdrew from them to his pavillion, which they soon surrounded; and, having there tired themselves with their acclamations, they kissed and embraced all the friends they met, and retired to spend the evening in mirth and feasting.

Titus soon made good by his actions what he had promised in his proclamation: he immediately dispatched *Lentulus* to *Asia*, to give freedom to the *Bargylians*; and *Titillius* to *Thrace*, to remove the garrisons of *Philip* from the towns and garrisons. *Publius Villius* went to treat with *Antiochus* about the freedom of the *Greeks* under him. *Titus* himself proceeded to *Chalcis*, and sailing from thence to *Magnesia*, removed the garrisons, and surrendered the government into the hands of the people. On his arrival at *Argos*, he was chosen judge of the *Nemean* games, an office which he executed to the satisfaction of all. He there proclaimed again the liberty of the *Grecians*; and, in all the cities through which he passed, he pressed the people to conform to their own laws; to adhere to the constant practice of justice, and to unite in the strictest friendship with the other states. He quelled the seditious, and those who had been banished he brought home. In short, his conquering *Philip* did not give him more pleasure than his success in reconciling *Greeks* with *Greeks*; and their liberty now seemed the least of the favours he had conferred upon them. The benefit

benefit *Rome* received from this generous conduct, did not consist only in empty praises; the power of the *Romans* became enlarged, and they deservedly gained the esteem and confidence of all nations; many of whom entreated to be under their government, and kings oppressed by kings, sought to be under their protection. *Titus* hung up some silver targets, together with his own shield, in the temple of *Delphi*, on which was an inscription, intimating that he had restored liberty to *Greece*: he also made an offering to *Apollo* of a golden crown.

Titus afterwards made war on *Nabis*, a most profligate and cruel tyrant of the *Spartans*: but he here disappointed the expectations of the *Grecians*, by concluding a peace with him when he might have taken him prisoner; but *Titus* alledged, that the tyrant's destruction would have been attended with the ruin of *Sparta*.

The *Achæans* decreed many honours to *Titus*; among which was a present that seemed equal to the greatness of his services. Those *Romans*, who, in the war with *Hannibal*, had the misfortune to be taken captive, being sold as slaves, were dispersed in various countries, and 1200 of them were at that time in *Greece*. This turn of fortune had justly rendered them objects of compassion, more particularly at that time, when some met their sons, some their brothers, and others their friends, who were freemen and conquerors, while they themselves were slaves.

Titus, though deeply concerned for them, took none of them by force from their masters: but the *Achæans* redeeming them at five *minæ* each, assembled them together, and made a present of them to him, just as he was going on board his ship; and he sailed away, filled with the highest satisfaction.

These afterwards formed the most glorious part of his triumph; for, as it is the custom for slaves, upon their manumission, to shave their heads, and wear a peculiar kind of caps, these redeemed *Romans* thus followed the triumphal chariot of *Titus*. To add to the splendor of this show, the *Grecian* helmets, the *Macedonian* targets and spears, with the rest of the spoils, were carried in pomp before him, together with vast quantities of gold and silver; for, according to *Itanus*, there were carried in his triumph 3713 pounds weight of unwrought gold, 43,270 of silver, 14,514 pieces of coined gold called *Philipicks*; besides which, *Philip* owed a thousand talents; though the *Romans*, chiefly by the mediation of *Titus*, remitted this debt, and declaring *Philip* their ally and confederate, sent home his son, who had been delivered up as an hostage.

Some time after *Antiochus*, with a numerous fleet and a powerful army, entered *Greece*, in order to prevail on the cities to engage in a war with the *Romans*; in which he was assisted by the *Ætolians*, who, for want of a more specious pretence, instructed him to colour his enterprize with the pleasing name of of liberty. The conful *Manlius Atilius* was fent to take the charge of the war, and *Titus*, out of refpect to the *Greeks*, was appointed his lieutenant. On his firft arrival, he confirmed the fidelity of thofe who were their friends, and prevented the defection of fuch as began to waver. A few had been fo wholly perverted by the *Ætolians*, that all his endeavours to gain them were ineffectual; yet, notwithftanding they had exafperated him, he granted them his protection when the battle was over; for *Antiochus* being defeated at *Thermopylæ*, fled, and fet fail for *Afia*.

After this, *Manlius* laid fiege to fome of the towns belonging to the *Ætolians*, while he abandoned others to king *Philip*. But *Titus* being touched with compaffion for *Greece*, came from the *Peloponnefus*, and reproached the conful for permitting king *Philip* to reap the whole profit of the war, when he himfelf had gained the victory; and for fpending his time in the fiege of *Naupactus*, which was then in the hands of the *Ætolians*, merely to gratify his anger, while the *Macedonians* over-ran feveral nations and kingdoms. *Titus* happening then to ftand in view of the befieged, they no fooner faw him, but calling to him from the wall, and ftretching forth their hands, implored his favour: but making them no reply, he turned with tears in his eyes, and went away; yet foon after, he prevailed on *Manlius* to grant the *Ætolians* a truce, and to allow them time to send deputies to *Rome*, to petition the senate for favourable terms. The *Chalcidians* having also justly offended *Manlius* by the respect they had shewn to *Antiochus*, he marched against them; but *Titus* followed him, in order to appease his resentment, and at length, by his entreaties, and a sedulous application to those of the greatest quality and interest in *Rome* succeeded.

The *Chalcidians* now expressed their gratitude to *Titus*, by dedicating to him the most magnificent of their public structures. Thus to this day may be seen the inscriptions, *The people dedicate this Gymnasium to* Titus *and to* Hercules; and *The people consecrate the Delphinium to* Titus *and to* Apollo. Even to this time they with great form elect a priest to *Titus*, and after the sacrifice with the libations are over, they sing an hymn to his honour; the conclusion of which is as follows:

The sons of Rome *with joy we trust;*
To all their vows minutely just.
To Jove, *ye* Muses, *raise the song;*
To Jove *and* Rome *your strains belong:*
The Roman *faith and* Titus *sing;*
Iö Titus! *Saviour! King!*

Honours were also heaped upon him by other parts of *Greece*, but what rendered them truly valuable, was the sincere affection of the people by whom they were bestowed, and which he had gained by his equity and moderation. For whenever he was at variance with any one, as was once the case with *Phi-lopœmen*, and with *Diaphenes*, general of the *Achæans*, his resentment never broke out into acts; but having vented itself in the freedom of discourse usual in public debates, it subsided. Though he often appeared hasty and passionate, no one ever found him implacable and revengeful: he was a most agreeable companion, and in his conversation, good sense was joined with much wit and pleasantry.

Titus on his return to *Rome*, after the conconclusion of the war with *Antiochus*, was created censor: an office of the highest dignity. The son of *Marcellus*, who had been five times consul, was his colleague. They expelled four of the senators, who were persons of inconsiderable note, and by the decree of the people, made in compliance with *Terentius Culeo*, their tribune, admitted all that offered themselves, to the privilege of *Roman* citizens, provided their parents were free.

Titus's natural ambition met with general applause, while the above wars afforded a proper occasion for its exertion: but when he was far advanced in years, he was highly censured for retaining still a violent thirst for fame. To some such disposition, his behaviour to *Hannibal* is thought to have been owing. *Hannibal* having fled his country, first took sanctuary with *Antiochus*; but after the battle in *Phrygia*, that prince being glad to conclude a peace with the *Romans*, Hannibal

nibal was obliged again to fly, and after wandering through many countries, found protection in the court of *Prusias*, king of *Bithynia*. His place of retreat was known at *Rome*; but he was considered as a man enfeebled by age, and one who had been cast off by fortune. But *Titus* being sent ambassador to that court, and seeing *Hannibal* there, could not bear his being suffered to live. And though *Prusias* used many intreaties in his favour, as an acquaintance, a friend, and a suppliant to whom he had granted his protection, *Titus* would take no denial *. There is a sandy place in *Bithynia*, bordering on the sea, near a little village named *Libyssa*; thither *Hannibal* chanced to retire, and having all along distrusted the ductile and easy temper of *Prusias*, and feared the resentment of the *Romans*, he had caused seven subterraneous passages to be dug under his house; these being continued far under ground, terminated in different places. Hearing therefore that *Titus* had ordered him to be seized, he attempted to make his escape through these caves, but finding them beset with the king's guards, he resolved to put a period to his life. Some

* This seems the most exceptionable passage in the life of this great man. It was little, it was mean and cowardly, thus to seek the life of a brave old man, whose greatest crime was, that he had once shewn, that he was inferior to no *Roman* in valour and ambition.

Hippias and *Androcleon*, three young men of approved loyalty, strength, and courage, who were to continue their flight, till they reached *Megara*, a town in *Macedonia*; while they themselves stopped the course of the pursuers, and having afterwards, with much difficulty got clear of them, they hastened to join those who had the care of *Pyrrhus*. But when the sun was ready to set, and they were near the accomplishment of their hopes, they were stopped by a river, which having been swelled by the rains was not fordable. The approaching darkness of the night added to their distress, and they despaired of conveying over the child and the woman who attended him, without farther assistance. Perceiving some of the inhabitants of the place on the other side; they called out for their help; but the roaring of the water prevented their being heard. At last one of them peeled off a piece of bark from an oak, and wrote upon it with the tongue of a buckle the necessities and fortunes of the child; then fastening it to a stone, threw it over to the other side: others say, that they fastened it to the end of a javelin, and darted it over. The people on the opposite shore having read what was on the bark, instantly cut down some trees, lashed them together, and came over to them; when the first who got ashore took the prince in his arms, and conveyed him over, while the rest performed the same service for his followers.

Having thus crossed the river, and got out of the reach of their enemies, they prosecuted their journey till they arrived at the court of *Glaucias*, king of *Illyria*, whom they found sitting in his palace with his queen, and imploring his protection, they laid the child at his feet. The king, who was under apprehensions from the power of *Cassander*, the mortal enemy of *Æacides*, remained silent, not knowing how to act. But at length, the child creeping towards him, laid hold of his robe, and raising himself on his feet, stood at his knees. The king at first laughed; but was soon touched with compassion for the helpless infant, who seemed to implore his protection. Others say, that the child crept to the altar of the Penates, and raising himself up, stretched out his arms, which made *Glaucias* consider the affair in a religious light. However, taking the infant in his arms, he delivered it to the queen, and ordered that he should be brought up with his own children. His enemies some time after sent to demand him, and *Cassander* offered the king 200 talents on condition of his delivering him up; but this *Glaucias* refused, and when he was twelve years of age, conducted him at the head of an army to *Epirus*, and placed him on the throne.

The countenance of *Pyrrhus* had an air of majesty more terrible than august. In his upper jaw he had no separate teeth, but a continued bone, marked with small lines that resembled the divisions of a row of them.

When

The Infant PYRRHUS laid at the Feet of GLAUCIAS King of Illyria.

When he was about seventeen years of age, and the government to appearance well settled, he left his kingdom in order to be present at the marriage of one of the sons of *Glaucias*, with whom he had been educated: but in his absence the *Molossians* expelled all of his party, rifled his treasury, and placed *Neoptolemus* on the throne.

Pyrrhus being thus deprived of his kingdom, applied to *Demetrius*, the son of *Antigonus*; and, at the great battle of *Ipsus*, in which all the kings of the earth * were engaged, accompanied *Demetrius*, and distinguished himself by his bravery. Afterwards, when *Demetrius*'s fortunes were low, he did not forsake him, but secured for him some of the *Grecian* cities with which he was entrusted. At length, on an agreement being concluded between *Demetrius* and *Ptolemy*, *Pyrrhus* was sent as an hostage into *Egypt*, where, in hunting and other exercises, he gave *Ptolemy* convincing proofs of his strength and courage. He there observed, that of all *Ptolemy*'s wives, *Berenice*, who was most esteemed for her virtue and understanding, had the greatest power, he therefore principally paid his court to her; for he had a peculiar art in recommending himself to the great, when it was necessary to promote his own interest,

* These kings were *Lysimachus*, *Cassander*, *Ptolemy*, *Seleucus*, *Demetrius*, and *Antigonus*, whom *Plutarch*, by an hyperbole, calls all the kings of the earth.

while

while he over-looked such as were below him. As he appeared to be endued with uncommon prudence and moderation, he, in preference to several other young princes, obtained in marriage *Antigone* the daughter of *Berenice*, by *Philip* her first husband; and by her means he obtained men and money which enabled him to recover his kingdom.

On his arrival at *Epirus*, his subjects, who hated *Neoptolemus* for his arbitrary and tyrannical government, received him with open arms; but *Pyrrhus* fearing lest that prince should have recourse to some other kings for assistance, chose to associate him in the kingdom: but this harmony was soon interrupted. It was customary for the kings of *Epirus* to hold an assembly at *Passaro*, a place in the province of the *Molossians*, where, having sacrificed to *Jupiter the Warrior*, the kings took an oath, by which they obliged themselves to govern according to law, and the people swore to maintain them in the government. At this time the ceremony was performed in the presence of the two kings and their friends, after which presents were made and received on both sides. Among the rest, *Gelon*, a friend of *Neoptolemus*, made *Pyrrhus* a present of two yoke of oxen; on which *Myrtilus*, *Pyrrhus*'s cup-bearer, begged them; but refusing him, he gave them to another. *Gelon* knowing that *Myrtilus* was highly offended at being refused this favour, invited him to supper, and after it was over, persuaded him to embrace the interest of *Neoptolemus*, and to poison

poison his master. This design *Myrtilus* seemed to approve, but immediately discovered it to *Pyrrhus*, who being desirous of having the crime proved by more than one evidence, directed him to take *Alexicrates*, his chief cup-bearer with him, and to recommend him to *Gelon*, as a fit instrument for their purpose. This being done, *Gelon* was so pleased, that he communicated his design to *Neoptolemus*, who not doubting of his friend's success, was unable to conceal his inhuman joy, but gave it vent among his friends; and in particular, revealed the whole affair to his sister *Cadmia*, while at supper with her, thinking none within hearing but themselves; but *Phænerete*, the wife of *Samon*, the chief keeper of *Neoptolemus*'s cattle, had laid herself on a couch, with her face turned towards the wall, and pretending to be fast asleep, heard all without suspicion, and the next day went and revealed it to *Antigone*. This was told to *Pyrrhus*, who seemed to take no notice of it; but one night, after the performance of a solemn sacrifice, he invited *Neoptolemus* to supper, and slew him; for all the leading men of *Epirus* were in *Pyrrhus*'s interest; they had often pressed him to remove *Neoptolemus* from the throne, and had now advised him to save his own life by taking his.

Pyrrhus, in acknowledgment of his obligations to *Ptolemy* and *Berenice*, gave the name of *Ptolemy* to a son he had by *Antigone*, and having built a city in the peninsula of

Epirus, he called it *Berenicis.* He began now to form great designs. *Antipater,* the eldest son of *Cassander,* had killed his mother *Thessalonica,* and expelled *Alexander* his brother from the throne of *Macedon;* on which *Alexander* applied to *Pyrrhus* for assistance, who marched to his aid; but demanded, as the reward of his services, the city of *Nymphæa,* all the maritime coast of *Macedonia,* with *Amphilochia, Acarnania,* and *Ambracia,* which were some of the conquered countries that did not anciently belong to the kingdom of *Macedonia.* The young prince complying with this demand, *Pyrrhus* took possession of those countries, secured them with good garrisons, and restored to *Alexander* the rest of the kingdom which he gained from *Antipater.*

The affairs of that prince were now settled; notwithstanding which, the arrival of *Demetrius,* who had before been invited to give him assistance, struck *Alexander* with terror; in a few days, mutual jealousies arose between them; they plotted against each other; and *Demetrius* seizing the first opportunity, murdered the young king, and then caused himself to be proclaimed king of *Macedon.*

There had been for some time no very good understanding between *Demetrius* and *Pyrrhus;* for the thirst of power and dominion rendered their neighbourhood uneasy and formidable to each other: besides, as each had seized on a part of *Macedonia,* their claims

now

now interfered with each other, and naturally afforded fresh subject for contention.

Demetrius having afterwards subdued the *Ætolians*, left *Pentauchus* with part of his forces to secure his conquests, and at the head of the rest, marched against *Pyrrhus*, who being informed that he was coming, went to meet him; but both mistaking the way, passed by each other. *Demetrius* ravaged *Epirus*, while *Pyrrhus* meeting *Pentauchus*, gave him battle. The dispute was on both sides warm and obstinate; for *Pentauchus*, who excelled all *Demetrius*'s officers in dexterity, strength, and courage, challenged *Pyrrhus* to single combat. On the other hand, *Pyrrhus*, who was inferior to none in fortitude and a thirst of glory, advanced against him thro' the front of the army. They first made use of their lances, and then of their swords, which they used with great strength and address. *Pyrrhus* received one wound, and his enemy two, which brought him to the ground, on which he was rescued by his friends. The *Epirots*, now elated with the victory of their king, and animated by his courage, broke and put to flight the *Macedonian* phalanx, pursued the fugitives with a great slaughter, and took 5000 prisoners. The very *Macedonians* could not help being astonished at the valour of *Pyrrhus*, or forbear thinking that in his countenance and impetuosity he resembled *Alexander* the Great.

Pyrrhus now returned home, exulting in the honour he had acquired. The *Epirots* called

called him their Eagle; on which he replied,
" 'Tis by your means that I am an Eagle;
" for what can I be less when I am borne up-
" on your arms, as on wings?"

Pyrrhus being some time after informed that *Demetrius* was dangerously ill, suddenly marched into *Macedonia*, intending only to ravage the country: but meeting with no opposition, he advanced as far as *Edessa*, the capital of the kingdom, without striking a blow; and, as he was joined by many of the inhabitants, was very near taking possession of the kingdom; but *Demetrius* and his friends soon raised a considerable army, and attacked *Pyrrhus* with all their forces, who coming only to pillage, declined the battle, though in his retreat he lost a part of his army.

Demetrius now forming great designs, and thinking of nothing less than recovering his father's dominions, with an army of ten thousand men and five hundred ships, was desirous of concluding a peace with *Pyrrhus*, that he might, with the greater safety, make use of his forces against the other kings. The conclusion of this peace was succeeded by such preparations as soon made known his designs. The kings were alarmed, and sent their ambassadors with letters to *Pyrrhus*, expressing their astonishment at his sitting still till his enemy was at leisure, and in a condition to attack him, notwithstanding he had been so lately deprived by *Demetrius* both of his wife and the city of *Corcyra*.

Lanissa,

Lanissa, one of *Pyrrhus*'s wives, and the daughter of *Agathocles* the *Syracusan*, had for her dowry *Corcyra*, which had been taken by her father; but she being offended at *Pyrrhus* for shewing greater tokens of love to his other wives than to her, withdrew to *Corcyra*; and being desirous of marrying some other king, made an overture to *Demetrius*, who sailing thither, espoused *Lanissa*, and placed a garrison in the island.

The kings having sent this advice to *Pyrrhus*, found work for *Demetrius* while he was making his preparations: *Ptolemy* set sail with a large fleet, and drew off many of the *Grecian* cities: *Lysimachus* marching from *Thrace*, laid waste the upper *Macedon*; and *Pyrrhus* taking arms at the same time, marched to *Berœa*, rightly judging, that *Demetrius*, by drawing his forces against *Lysimachus*, would leave the lower country defenceless. He with long marches reached *Berœa*, which he took, and made his head quarters, reducing the rest of the country by his commanders. *Demetrius* receiving intelligence of this, and perceiving that his army was ready to mutiny, was afraid to advance farther against *Lysimachus*, lest his troops should revolt to him, on account of his being a *Macedonian* distinguished for his bravery. He therefore returned, and marching against *Pyrrhus*, encamped with his forces near *Berœa*.

While he lay there, many of the inhabitants came out of the city to visit their friends

friends in the camp, where they highly praised *Pyrrhus*, as an illustrious prince, invincible in arms, who treated all that fell into his hands with great tenderness and humanity. *Pyrrhus* also privately sent others to the camp, who pretending to be *Macedonians*, said, that now was the time for them to deliver themselves from the cruelty of *Demetrius*, by declaring for *Pyrrhus*, a popular prince, who shewed great kindness to his soldiers. This had the desired effect; the greatest part of the army cast their eyes to the enemy's camp to see if they could discover *Pyrrhus*. At that instant his helmet happened to be off; but immediately recollecting himself, he put it on, and was in a moment known by his glittering plume, and crest of goat's horns. On which the *Macedonians* running in a turbulent manner, desired *Demetrius* to come to an agreement with *Pyrrhus*; while others put oaken boughs on their heads, because they saw them worn by the soldiers of *Pyrrhus*; and some had even the confidence to tell *Demetrius*, that it would be for his interest to withdraw and lay down the government. Upon this *Demetrius* privately fled, disguised in a mean coat and a *Macedonian* hat; on which *Pyrrhus*, without fighting, became master of the camp, and was declared king of the *Macedonians*.

But soon after *Lysimachus* arriving, affirmed that he had contributed as much to the flight and expulsion of *Demetrius* as *Pyrrhus*, and that therefore the kingdom ought to be
shared

shared between them: when *Pyrrhus* not being well assured of the fidelity of the *Macedonians*, consented, and they divided the cities and provinces between them. This prevented a war; but they soon found that this partition, instead of terminating all disputes, proved an occasion of mutual complaint and dissention. For how was it possible, that princes whose ambition can neither be bounded by seas, mountains, nor uninhabited desarts, should, when so near to each other, rest contented with their possessions, and abstain from injustice and violence? Peace and war they employ not as justice directs, but use them indifferently, like pieces of money, to suit their present interest. They are more worthy of esteem when they openly make war, than when they give to the want of opportunity to do wrong, the sacred names of justice and friendship.

Pyrrhus soon renewed his opposition to *Demetrius*, who began to recover his affairs, as strength returns after sickness; he marched to the assistance of the *Grecians*, and entering the city of *Athens*, went up to the citadel, where he sacrificed to *Minerva*; but returning to the city, told the *Athenians* that he was highly pleased with the affection they had shewn, and the confidence they had placed in him; but that if they were wise, they would never suffer any king to enter their city. Soon after he concluded a peace with *Demetrius*; but yet, on his passing into *Asia*,

Asia, he, by the persuasion of *Lysimachus*, prevailed on the *Thessalians* to revolt, and to keep his *Macedonian* subjects employed, attacked the garrisons he had in *Greece*.

At length, while *Pyrrhus* was with his troops, which were quartered at *Edessa*, *Lysimachus*, having no other employment for his arms, marched against him, and on his advancing near that city, took one of the king's convoys, which distressed the army with the want of provisions; then by letters and false rumours he corrupted the chief of the *Macedonian* officers, whom he reproached for having chosen for their sovereign a stranger, while they expelled the old friends and companions of *Alexander* from the country. These representations had soon such an effect upon the rest of the *Macedonians*, that *Pyrrhus* fearing the event, withdrew with his *Epirots* and auxiliary forces, losing *Macedon* in the same manner as that by which he had gained it. Thus kings have no reason to condemn the fickleness of the people, since they do but imitate them, who are their instructors in treachery and perfidy.

Pyrrhus now returned to *Epirus*, where fortune gave him a fair opportunity of enjoying himself in quiet, and peaceably governing his own subjects; but he thought life insupportably tedious unless he was doing mischief to others, or repelling it when offered to him, and therefore readily seized the following opportunity of obtaining a fresh opportunity for doing it.

The

The *Tarentines* were at this time at war with the *Romans*, but being unable either to support or conclude it, on account of the bold and turbulent speeches of their leading men, they resolved to call in *Pyrrhus* and make him their general. The graver and more discreet citizens opposed this advice, but were over-borne by the noise and violence of the multitude. On the day when this public decree was to be ratified, and the people were all seated, *Meton*, a very worthy man, came dancing into the assembly like one drunk, with a wither'd garland on his head, a torch in his hand, and a woman before him playing on a flute; as in those popular assemblies, no decorum was observed, some clapped their hands, others laughed, and others called on her to play, and him to sing; but when silence was made, *Meton*, instead of singing, cried, " 'Tis well done of
" you, O *Tarentines!* not to hinder any from
" making themselves merry, while it is yet
" in their power; if you are wise, you will
" still preserve this freedom; for you must
" change your course of life, when *Pyrrhus*
" comes." These words made a strong impression on many of the *Tarentines*; but some who feared their being sacrificed to the *Romans* if a peace was made, reproached the assembly for listening to a drunkard, and crowding upon him, thrust him out. Thus the decree was passed, and ambassadors were sent to *Epirus*, both in their own name and in that of the *Italian Greeks*, carrying presents

sents to *Pyrrhus*, and having orders to tell him, that they wanted only a general of his fame and experience; they being able to raise a powerful army of *Messapians*, *Lucanians*, *Samnites*, and *Tarentines*, amounting to no less than 20,000 horse, and 350,000 foot. This not only animated *Pyrrhus*, but also inspired the *Epirots* with a strong inclination to the war.

At that time *Pyrrhus* had at his court *Cineas* a *Thessalian*, who had been a disciple of *Demosthenes*, and was esteemed the only orator of his time, who could revive in the minds of his hearers, a strong idea of the force and eloquence of his master. *Pyrrhus* had therefore employed him in several embassies, and used to say, that *Cineas* had taken more towns with his words, than he with his arms; whence he treated him with great respect, and employed him in the most important affairs. *Cineas* finding *Pyrrhus* intent on preparing for this war, seized the opportunity of a leisure hour, and drew him insensibly into the following conversation. The *Romans*, said he, have the reputation of being excellent soldiers, and govern many warlike nations: if we have the good fortune to conquer them, what benefits shall we reap from our victory? *Cineas*, replied the king, when once we have conquered the *Romans*, there will be no town in all the country able to oppose us. We shall at once be masters of all *Italy*, whose riches, strength and power are better known to thee than to any other man.

And

And having subdued *Italy*, continued *Cineas*, after a short pause, What shall we do next? *Sicily*, a rich and populous island, he replied, holds out her arms to receive us, and may be easily gained; for faction and anarchy prevail in all their towns, and every thing is at the discretion of the turbulent orators. That is highly probable, said *Cineas*, but shall the possession of *Sicily* put an end to the war? Far from it, cried *Pyrrhus*; for if fortune favours us with victory there, that shall be only the fore-runner of greater undertakings; for when *Sicily* is reduced, who can forbear *Lybia* and *Carthage*, then within our reach? And when we have added *Africa* to our conquests, certainly none of the enemies who now disturb us will dare to make any farther resistance. No, replied *Cineas*; for when we are arrived at such mighty power, we shall soon recover *Macedon*, and govern *Greece* without controul. But when we have conquered all, what are we to do next? Why then, my friend, replied *Pyrrhus* laughing, we will live at our ease, drink and be merry. *Cineas* having brought him thus far, hastily returned; And what hinders us now from living at our ease, and indulging mirth and pleasure? We have already at hand what we are going to seek at the expence of so much blood, fatigue, and treasure; and of so many calamities, which we ourselves shall suffer, and which we shall inflict upon others.

Pyrrhus

Pyrrhus was, however, rather afflicted than corrected by this discourse; for though he was convinced that he was foregoing a certain happiness, he could not abandon his favourite hopes: he therefore detached *Cineas* with 3000 foot to *Tarentum*; and soon after there arrived from thence a great number of transports, gallies, and flat bottomed boats, on board of which he embarked twenty elephants, 3000 horse, 20,000 foot, 2000 archers, and 500 slingers.

Pyrrhus, with this fleet, was no sooner out at sea, than he was overtaken by a violent storm; but, by the great skill and resolution of his officers and seamen, they with infinite labour made the *Italian* shore. The rest of the fleet were however dispersed. While the wind blew from the sea, the king's ship, by its bulk and strength, resisted the force of the waves; but the wind changing, and blowing directly from the shore, and the vessel keeping up with its head against it, was in danger of opening by the shocks it received, or of being driven out to sea, which continued very tempestuous. In this extremity, *Pyrrhus* leap'd over-board, and was instantly followed by his friends and guards, earnestly contending who should give him most assistance; but the darkness of the night, and the violence of the storm, rendered it exceeding difficult to save him: however, the wind being considerably laid by day-break, he with much difficulty got ashore, extremely weakened and fatigued. At the same time the

the *Messapians*, on whose coast he was thrown, ran to render him all the service in their power, and met with some straggling vessels that had escaped the storm; in which were a few horses, two elephants, and not quite 2000 foot, with which *Pyrrhus* marched towards *Tarentum*; when *Cineas* being informed of his approach, drew out his forces to meet him.

Pyrrhus, on his first arrival, did not give the least offence to the *Tarentines*; but hearing that all his ships were safe in the harbour, and being joined by the best part of his army, he began to change his conduct. He found that the citizens intended to remain idle at home, and to spend their time in bathing, feasting, and idle diversions, while he was fighting for them in the field. But this he would not suffer; he deprived them of their feasts and shews; called the youth to arms, and treated with the most inflexible severity, such as did not appear at the musters and military exercises; so that many who were unaccustomed to such exact discipline, left the city, thinking that their not being suffered to enjoy a voluptuous life was the most insupportable slavery.

Pyrrhus now receiving advice, that *Lævinus* the *Roman* consul was marching towards him with a powerful army, and that he was already laying waste *Lucania*, thought it a disgrace to sit still; and though the confederate troops were not arrived, took the field; but before he marched, sent an herald to the *Romans*,

mans, to propose terminating their differences with the *Greeks* of *Italy*, by allowing him to be umpire between them; but *Lævinus* told the herald, That the *Romans* would neither accept *Pyrrhus* for an arbiter, nor feared him as an enemy.

The king having received this answer, advanced with his troops; encamped in the plain between the cities of *Pandosia* and *Heraclea*; and hearing that the *Romans* were encamped very near him, on the other side of the river *Siris*, he mounted on horseback, and rode up to take a view of them: when seeing the appearance of their troops, their advanced guards, the fine order that universally prevailed, and the happy disposition of their camp, he was surprized, and turning to one of his friends who was near him; "*Megacles*, said he, the dispositions of these Barbarians are by no means barbarous; we shall see how the rest will answer this appearance." This rendering him somewhat more doubtful of the event, he resolved to wait the arrival of the confederates, and lest the *Romans* should in the mean time cross the river, he planted troops along the banks to dispute their passage: but they resolving to attack him before the arrival of the forces he expected, attempted the passage with their infantry where it was fordable, the horse getting over where they could. So that the *Greeks* on its banks dreading their being surrounded, were obliged to retreat.

Pyrrhus

Pyrrhus, much concerned at this news, immediately ordered the foot to form and stand to their arms, while he advanced at the head of the horse, who amounted to about 3000, hoping he should still be able to dispute the passage of the river: but seeing a vast number of shields glittering above the water, and the horse advancing in good order, he drew up his men into a closer body and began the charge. He was soon known by the beauty and lustre of his armour, which was exceeding rich, and by his actions shewed that the reputation he had acquired did not exceed his merit. For though he exposed his person in the engagement, and fought with the greatest bravery, his mind was still free and undisturbed, and he gave his orders with the utmost care and prudence; flying from place to place, and assisting those whom he thought most pressed by the enemy.

In the heat of the action, *Leonatus*, a *Macedonian*, observing one of the *Italian* cavalry solely intent upon *Pyrrhus*, and following him every where with great ardour, said to him, "Do you see, Sir, that Barbarian on the black horse? he seems filled with some great design: his eyes are fixed on thee: he appears to aim at no one else; for all his fury appears levelled at thee alone. Take care of him." "*Leonatus*, said *Pyrrhus*, it is impossible for any man to avoid his fate; but neither he, nor any other *Italian*, shall gain much by engaging me." While they were holding this discourse, the *Italian* poising his lance, and clapping spurs to his horse, rode full against *Pyrrhus*; but missing him, killed his horse, as *Leonatus* did the *Italian*'s, so that they both fell together. *Pyrrhus* was instantly surrounded by a crowd of his friends, who carrying him off, killed the *Italian*, who died fighting with the utmost bravery.

This adventure taught *Pyrrhus* to use more caution, and to take more care of his person; and now seeing his cavalry give ground, he brought up his infantry, gave his robe and his armour to *Megacles*, one of his friends, and disguising himself in his, vigorously charged the *Romans*, who made a brave resistance: the success of the battle remained long doubtful; and it is said that each army seven times gave way, and as often returned to the charge.

Pyrrhus changed his arms very opportunely for saving his life; but, on the other hand, it almost lost him the victory; for the enemy rushed in crowds upon *Megacles*; and *Dexius*, who first wounded and overthrew him, seizing his robe and helmet, rode full speed to *Lævinus*, crying that he had slain *Pyrrhus*. These spoils were immediately carried through the ranks, and the cries of victory now resounded on all sides, while the army of the *Greeks* were filled with consternation. But *Pyrrhus* perceiving the mistake, ran through his lines, with his face uncovered, holding out his hands to his soldiers, and making himself known by his voice and gestures.

gestures. The battle being renewed, the elephants at last principally determined the victory; for the horses, unable to bear the sight of them even at a distance, recoiled back with their riders; when *Pyrrhus* ordering the *Thessalian* cavalry to charge the *Romans* while in this disorder, gave them a total overthrow. According to *Dionysius* of *Halicarnassus* near 15,000 of the *Romans* were slain; but *Hieronymus* computes their loss to be only 7000. On *Pyrrhus*'s side, *Dionysius* says, there were 13,000 slain; *Hieronymus* makes them less than 4000; but they were the flower of his troops, among whom were his chief friends, and his best officers, in whom he most confided, and whom he always employed on important occasions.

Immediately *Pyrrhus* seized the *Roman* camp which he found abandoned; and without losing time drew off several of their confederate cities, wasted the country all around, and advanced within thirty-seven miles of *Rome*. After the battle, he was joined by the *Lucanians* and *Samnites*, whom he sharply reproved for their delay; yet it plainly appeared that he secretly rejoiced that he had defeated so great an army of the *Romans* with no other assistance but that of the *Tarentines*.

Notwithstanding this defeat, the *Romans* would not recall *Lævinus* their consul; tho' they were told by *Fabricius*, that the *Romans* were not defeated by the *Epirots*, but *Lævinus* by *Pyrrhus*. They immediately raised fresh

fresh forces; at which the king being a-
mazed, resolved to try whether they were
disposed to conclude a peace; for he now
thought it impossible with such an army as
his to make himself master of *Rome*. He sent
Cineas on this errand to that city, who had a
conference with the chief men of *Rome*, to
each of whom he gave presents from the king,
and also to their wives; but they all refused
them, the women, as well as the men declaring, that at the conclusion of the peace,
they would readily give the king all possible
demonstrations of their respect. *Cineas*
being admitted to an audience of the senate, made a speech, in which he endeavoured in a graceful manner to incline them
to an accommodation. But, though *Pyrrhus*
had offered to release the prisoners without
ransom, and to assist the *Romans* in the entire
conquest of *Italy*; desiring nothing in return
but their friendship, and security for the *Tarentines*, they rejected his proposals. There
were some indeed who seemed inclined to a
peace; but *Appius Claudius*, who on account
of his great age and loss of sight, had retired
from public affairs, hearing of the king's
offers, and that it was probable they would
be accepted, could not contain himself, but
causing his servants to carry him in his chair
to the senate-house, was set down at the door,
and led in by his son. At his appearance,
the whole assembly observed a respectful
silence, and he spoke to the following purpose: " Till now, O *Romans!* I have con-
" sidered

"sidered my loss of sight as a misfortune;
"but you have brought me to wish that I
"was as deaf as I am blind, that I might
"not hear the shameful resolutions, by
"which you would efface all the glory of
"*Rome*. Where are your boasts, that if *A-*
"*lexander* the Great had invaded *Italy*, and
"turned his arms against us, he would not
"now have been called invincible; but
"either by his flight or his death, would
"have added fresh glory to the *Roman*
"name? How vain were these boasts?
"Are you not afraid of the *Molossians* and
"*Chaonians?* Of those who were always
"conquered by the *Macedonians?* You trem-
"ble at the name of *Pyrrhus*, who has been
"educated in a dependance on one of *Alex-*
"*ander*'s guards. Hither he is come less to
"succour the *Greeks* who dwell amongst us,
"than to escape from his enemies at home;
"and has the insolence to promise us the
"conquest of *Italy* with the very army with
"which he was unable to preserve a small
"part of *Macedon*. But your entering into
"an alliance with him, will only open a
"door to new invaders, who will consider
"you as an easy conquest, if *Pyrrhus* es-
"capes without being punished for his pre-
"sumption."

Appius no sooner ceas'd speaking, than they unanimously voted for the continuance of the war; telling *Cineas*, That when *Pyrrhus* had drawn his forces out of *Italy*, they should be ready to enter into an alliance with him; but while he staid there in arms, they would prosecute

secute the war against him, though he should defeat a thousand *Lævinuses*. It is said, that while *Cineas* was there, he made it his business to study the manners of the *Romans*, and afterwards difcourfing with *Pyrrhus* on that subject, he told him, That the senate seemed like an assembly of kings; and that the people were so numerous, that he feared they had to do with another Hydra : for *Lævinus* had already an army twice as large as the former, and yet had left in *Rome* an infinite number of *Romans* capable of bearing arms.

Fabricius being afterwards sent ambassador to *Pyrrhus*, to treat of the ransom of the prisoners, *Cineas* told that prince that tho' he was very poor, he was revered by the *Romans* for his virtue, and was an excellent soldier. *Pyrrhus* received him with great kindness, and offered him some gold, not to engage him in any dishonourable design, but as a pledge of his friendship. *Fabricius* refusing to accept it, he pressed him no farther; but being willing to try whether he was as intrepid as he was difinterested, and knowing that he had never seen an elephant, he the next day had one of the largest compleatly armed, placed behind a curtain in the room where they held their conference; when upon a sign given, the curtain was drawn aside, and the elephant raising his trunk over *Fabricius*'s head, made a frightful noise. But *Fabricius* turning about, said with a smile, " Neither your gold yesterday, nor your
" elephant

" elephant to-day, can make any impref-
" fion on me."

That evening the difcourfe at table turned on the affairs of *Greece*, and particularly on the different fects of philofophers. *Cineas* dwelt particularly on the *Epicureans*, obferving that they placed the chief happinefs of man in pleafure, and attributed to the gods neither love nor hatred, maintaining, that they were perfectly regardlefs of human affairs, and lived whole ages in total inactivity, plunged in an eternal circle of pleafures. But while *Cineas* was ftill fpeaking, *Fabricius* cried out, " O heavens! may *Pyrrhus* and " the *Samnites* hold this doctrine as long as " they are at war with the *Romans*." His virtue and greatnefs of mind filled *Pyrrhus* with fuch admiration, that he became more defirous than ever of being the friend rather than the enemy of the *Romans*; and, in a private conference, endeavoured to perfuade *Fabricius* to procure a peace between him and that people, and then to fettle in his court, where he fhould be his moft intimate friend, and the chief of his generals. But though all his arguments were ineffectual, he was fo far from being offended, that he entrufted the prifoners to *Fabricius*, on condition that if the fenate refufed to conclude a peace, they fhould be fent back, after they had vifited their friends and relations, and celebrated the *Saturnalia*. Accordingly, after that feftival they were fent back, the fenate having decreed,

creed, that if any staid behind they should suffer death.

Fabricius was consul the following year, and was at the head of the army, when he received a letter from *Pyrrhus*'s physician, in which he offered, on condition of his receiving a reward proportionable to his service, to poison *Pyrrhus*, and thus put an end to the war without hazard to the *Romans*. But shocked at the baseness of this proposal, he by the consent of *Quintus Æmilius*, his colleague, wrote to *Pyrrhus* to inform him of the villainy of his physician; who having made strict enquiry into his treason, had him executed, and in return for the generosity of the *Romans*, sent the prisoners to *Rome* without ransom, and again commissioned *Cineas* to negociate a peace. In return, the *Romans* being unwilling to receive an obligation from an enemy, or a reward for not having complied with so base a proposal, returned him an equal number of the *Samnites* and *Tarentines:* but would not suffer *Cineas* to mention a peace, till *Pyrrhus* had sailed back with his forces to *Epirus*.

Pyrrhus finding it impossible to avoid a second engagement, attacked the *Romans* near *Asculum*, where he suffered much from the unevenness of the ground, and its being covered with wood, which was inconvenient to the cavalry, and entirely prevented the elephants from coming up with the infantry. Thus he lost many of his men, and had great numbers wounded. Night put an end to the battle.

PYRRHUS. 203

battle. But the next day, resolving to engage on a more even and open spot, he sent early in the morning to take possession of the incommodious post where he had engaged the day before: then drawing up his army, and disposing a great number of slingers and archers among his elephants, marched in good order against the enemy.

After a long and obstinate fight, the *Romans* were forced to give ground, particularly in that part where *Pyrrhus* fought in person; so strong was the impression he made at the head of his phalanx. But what chiefly contributed to their defeat, was the weight and force of the elephants, which bore down all before them. As the battle was fought at no great distance from their camp, they soon reach'd it. In this action *Hieronymus* says, the *Romans* lost 6000 men, and *Pyrrhus*, according to his own commentaries, no more than 3505. But *Dionysius* of *Halicarnassus* mentions only one engagement, which he says lasted till the sun was down: he observes, that *Pyrrhus* was wounded in the arm by a javelin; that his baggage was plundered by the *Samnites*; that the armies separated at night with great unwillingness, and that there were about 15,000 killed on both sides.

Both armies being retired, *Pyrrhus* was congratulated on his victory; upon which he replied, Such another will undo us; for he had indeed lost the greatest part of the forces he had brought out of *Epirus*, and almost all his particular friends, while the confederates were

were very slow in joining him. But the *Roman* camp was continually supplied, as from a fountain, with fresh troops flowing out of the city.

While he was in the midst of these difficulties, ambassadors arrived from *Sicily* to desire him to expel their tyrants, and drive the *Carthaginians* out of the island, offering to surrender to him *Syracuse*, *Agrigentum*, and the city of the *Leontines*. At the same time he received news from *Greece*, that *Ptolemy Ceraunus* having some time before been slain in battle by the *Gauls*, the *Macedonians* were not averse to his being their king. He now began to accuse fortune for giving him, at the same instant, two such glorious opportunities of action, since if he laid hold on one, he must necessarily relinquish the other. After much deliberation, he chose the *Sicilian* expedition, which he imagined, afforded the largest field of glory. He instantly dispatched *Cineas* to treat with the cities, and prepare them for his arrival. Mean while he placed a strong garrison in *Tarentum*, though the inhabitants endeavoured to persuade him to stay and continue the war with the *Romans*, or to leave the city as he found it.

On his arrival in *Sicily*, the cities readily submitted to him, and wherever his arms were necessary, he carried all before him; for with 30,000 foot, 2500 horse, and 200 ships, he entirely vanquished the *Phœnicians*, and overturned their government. *Eryx* the strongest town in their possession, having
a good

a good garrison, he resolved to take it by storm. When his army was ready to give the assault, he put on his armour, and placing himself at the head of his troops, vowed, in case he was victorious to offer sacrifices and games in honour of *Hercules*. Then giving the signal by sound of trumpet, he with a shower of arrows drove the Barbarians from the walls, planted his ladders, and was himself the first who mounted them. He was there attacked by a multitude of enemies, some of whom he drove back, others he threw down head-long on each side, while those he slew with his sword lay in heaps around him; and yet he escaped without a wound. The city was taken, after which he offered a magnificent sacrifice to *Hercules*, and exhibited shews and combats.

The *Mamertines*, who inhabited the city of *Messina*, were of all the Barbarians, those who most oppressed the *Greeks*; they having render'd the greatest part of them tributary: but *Pyrrhus* seizing their collectors, put them to death; he afterwards defeated the *Mamertines* in a pitched battle, and destroyed most of their towns. The *Carthaginians* at length offered to pay a sum of money, and to furnish him with ships, on condition of his concluding a peace with them; but he resolved to grant this on no other terms, but their abandoning *Sicily*, and making the *Libyan* sea the boundary between them and the *Greeks*.

Elated with his surprizing success, he now resolved to pursue the plan, for the sake of which

which he had engaged in this expedition. His chief aim was against *Africa*, where he intended to extend his victorious arms. He had hitherto endeavoured by kindness to gain the affections of the *Sicilians*, and placing an entire confidence in them, abstained from all violence and oppression; but now he endeavoured to man his fleet for his *African* expedition, by forcing the inhabitants into his service, and he was soon reproached with cruelty, falshood and ingratitude. But what chiefly alienated them from him was his behaviour to *Thonon* and *Sostratus*, who had greater authority than any other persons in *Syracuse*. At their invitation, he first set sail for *Sicily*; they had surrendered the city to him at his arrival, and were afterwards his principal agents. Yet growing jealous of them, he was unwilling either to take them with him, or to suffer them to stay behind. *Sostratus* dreading what might happen, made his escape; but *Thonon* being seized, was accused by *Pyrrhus* of being an accomplice with *Sostratus*, and put him to death. This at once ruined his affairs; for the cities on this account conceived such an hatred against him, that some of them admitted the *Carthaginians*; and others entered into a confederacy against him with the *Mamertines*.

While *Pyrrhus* was under the apprehensions that this defection would become general, he received letters from the *Samnites* and *Tarentines*, informing him that they had been twice defeated, and being unable to defend

defend their towns againſt the *Romans*, earneſtly entreated him to come to their aſſiſtance. Theſe letters furniſhing him with an honourable pretence for leaving *Sicily*, he abandoned that iſland, which he could no longer keep; when the Barbarians entering into a confederacy againſt him, he was attacked and defeated by a *Carthaginian* fleet in his paſſage, and after loſing many of his ſhips, was obliged to fly with the reſt to *Italy*; where 10,000 *Mamertines* having paſſed over before him, lay in wait in ſome narrow paſſes. Upon his arrival, he was attacked by this body, and his whole army put into confuſion. On this occaſion he loſt two of his elephants, and great part of his rear was cut to pieces. He immediately advanced in perſon from the van to their aſſiſtance, and diſtinguiſhed himſelf with ſurprizing valour againſt men who were perſonally exaſperated, and by long practice were trained to war. A wound in his hand forced him to retire a little from the place of action: this gave freſh courage to the *Mamertines*; one of whom, of an amazing ſize, and ſplendidly armed, advanced before the ranks, and with a loud and diſdainful voice, challenged the king, if he was yet alive, to come forth. Enraged at this challenge, *Pyrrhus* returned, attended by his guards, ſtorming with rage, and all over beſmeared with blood, he pierced through his battalions, and ruſhing upon the Barbarian, without allowing him time to defend himſelf, gave him ſuch a blow, as clove him down to the very seat. At which the Barbarians, struck with astonishment, considered him as something more than mortal, and retired.

Pyrrhus now continued his march without opposition, and arrived at *Tarentum*, with 20,000 foot and 3000 horse; where re-inforcing himself with a chosen body of the *Tarentine* troops, he immediately advanced against the *Romans*, who were encamped in the territories of the *Samnites*; and dividing his army into two parts, sent the first into *Lucania* to oppose one of the consuls there, in order to prevent his assisting his colleague, while he himself marched in person against *Manius Curius* the other consul, who was advantageously encamped near *Beneventum*, waiting for reinforcements. *Pyrrhus*, eager to engage him before he was joined by these, draughted out the best of his troops, and chusing the boldest and strongest of his elephants, marched by night towards the *Roman* camp: but being forced to take a circuit through a woody country, his lights failed him, and his soldiers lost their way in the dark. This obliged him to halt, in order to rally them, and his approach was discovered by the *Romans*. The consul drawing a body of troops out of the trenches, charged and routed the vanguard. Encouraged by this success, he drew out his whole army, and engaging *Pyrrhus* in a pitch'd battle, defeated one of his wings, while the other was borne down by the elephants, and forced back to
the

the trenches. The conful then ordering a body he had left to guard the camp to advance, they rush'd forward, wounded the elephants with their darts, and driving them back on *Pyrrhus*'s battalions, threw them into such confusion, that the *Romans* obtained a compleat victory.

Though *Pyrrhus* thus loft all his *Italian* and *Sicilian* hopes, after his having spent six years in these wars, yet he preserved his courage amidst all his misfortunes. He returned to *Epirus* with 8000 foot, and 500 horse; but his want of money now made him seek for another war in order to maintain them. Being joined by a body of *Gauls*, he invaded *Macedon*, where *Antigonus*, the son of *Demetrius*, then reigned. His first design was only to ravage the country; but having taken several towns, and being joined by 2000 of the inhabitants, he marched against *Antigonus*, and surprizing him in a narrow pass, threw his whole army into disorder; and a numerous body of *Gauls* who brought up *Antigonus*'s rear, were most of them cut to pieces, and all *Antigonus*'s elephants were taken. At length, *Pyrrhus* stretching out his hand, called aloud to the officers of the *Macedonian* phalanx, and prevailed both on them and the whole body of the infantry to desert *Antigonus*, who was thus forced to fly, and endeavour to keep the possession of some of the maritime towns.

This victory was succeeded by *Pyrrhus*'s taking several cities, among which was *Ægæ*, into which he put a garrison, consisting of some of the *Gauls* who had served in his army: but they were no sooner in possession of the place, than they dug up the tombs of the kings, seized on all the wealth that had been buried with them, and with insolent contempt scattered about their bones. *Pyrrhus* did not seem at all offended at this ignominious insult; perhaps deferring his resentment till a more proper time; but by this he lost his credit with the *Macedonians*.

About this time, *Cleonymus* coming to solicit *Pyrrhus* to replace him on the throne of *Sparta*, he marched with an army of 20,000 foot, 2000 horse, and 24 elephants. These extraordinary preparations rendered it evident that he came not so much to gain *Sparta* for *Cleonymus*, as to take all *Peloponnesus* for himself: yet this he expressly denied to the *Lacedæmonian* ambassadors who met him on the road. But he no sooner entered *Laconia*, than he began to ravage the country: when the ambassadors complaining that these acts of hostility were committed without a declaration of war, he replied, You *Lacedæmonians* never make public proclamation of your intentions? At which a *Spartan*, who was present, answered in the *Laconic* dialect:
" If thou art a god, thou wilt do us no harm,
" because we have done thee none; and if
" thou art a man, we may find others as
" strong as thee."

Pyrrhus in the mean time continued his march towards *Lacedæmon*, and was advised

www.ingramcontent.com/pod-product-compliance
Lightning Source LLC
Chambersburg PA
CBHW021810230426
43669CB00008B/694